SOUNDSTORM

SOUNDSTORM

MUSINGS ON THE MADNESS OF THE MODERN MUSIC ECOSYSTEM

SARANSH DESAI-CHOWDHRY

NEW DEGREE PRESS

COPYRIGHT © 2020 SARANSH DESAI-CHOWDHRY

All rights reserved.

SOUNDSTORM

Musings on the Madness of the Modern Music Ecosystem

ISBN

978-1-63676-628-7   *Paperback*
978-1-63676-255-5   *Kindle Ebook*
978-1-63676-257-9   *Digital Ebook*

For New York City, and for my parents

CONTENTS

INTRODUCTION
Weathering the Soundstorm, Together   11

MUSIC'S MYTHIC NIGHT
Dreams and Disillusionment at the Grammys   17

IDEALISTIC INELASTICITY
Bursting the Ticketing Bubble   37

DON'T CALL BLU DETIGER AN OVERNIGHT SUCCESS
Discipline and Detours in the Digital Age   47

THE SPOTIFY DILEMMA
Music's Messiest Divorce   59

MOURNING MY RECORD STORES
The Lineage of the Local Music Economy   73

PRESERVING MAGIC, PROTECTING LIVELIHOODS
Beyond New Orleans' Musical Escapes   87

FALSE INHERITANCE
The Oversaturation of the Self-Titled Album   97

BOLLYWOOD, CALIFORNIA
Navigating Cultural Appropriation as an ABCD   101

WHY BLAME BILLIE EILISH?
Confronting the Convention of Industry Planting   115

K-POP THE POLYLITH
Cultural Empathy through Commercial Escapism   131

JON & POP
Community Formation through Pop Music   145

SEIZING THE SUBJECTIVE
The Evolution of Music Criticism   161

AFTER LAUGHTER, AFTERMATH
Revisiting Music in Crisis   175

EPILOGUE
Listen to What You Love, Carry Your Own Umbrella   183

ACKNOWLEDGMENTS   193

APPENDIX   197

ABOUT THE AUTHOR   211

"Ambling down a city street with headphones on—you know, maybe it's dusk, maybe it's midsummer, maybe you had a really nice day—is, without a doubt, one of life's simplest and most perfect joys. ... We are all the lone stars of secret films, narrated by and in our own minds, and we seek out music that validates that position: separate, but forever plugged in."

—AMANDA PETRUSICH,
"HEADPHONES EVERYWHERE," *THE NEW YORKER*

INTRODUCTION

Weathering the Soundstorm, Together

The modern music ecosystem is a realm defined by rapid change, chaos, and unpredictability. It is a garden plot prone to natural and artificial disasters, though constantly seeded to produce the sweetest and most stimulating periods of flourishment.

People have written a lot about trends and patterns in music, but such work has almost always been done within entirely distinct silos. Through this collection of essays, I hope to bridge the gap between the business-oriented, creative and cultural words of music as the ecosystem experiences unprecedented growth and unforeseen challenges.

The music ecosystem comprises not just the music industry, but also all of the adjacent communities enveloping it—music education, criticism, governance, technology, and several other fields equally important in determining how music is made and how it ultimately penetrates the soundscape and our eardrums. As I see it, the lack of communication between these factions is a critical error resulting in countless disputes over decades, many personal, many legal.

In this book, I will not be your weatherman. I will not be your psychic or strategic forecaster. Instead, I will be your oversharing tour guide. Together, we will scale mountains, wade through rivers, admire ancient geysers, question the efficacy of greenhouses, and forge new pathways. We will weather the storm—the *sound*storm—together.

According to a June 2019 Goldman Sachs report, global music revenues will hit $131 billion by 2030.[1] However, in the wake of the coronavirus crisis, tours have been postponed indefinitely, executives have been furloughed, and many artists have lost their instruments, their jobs, and even their homes to make up for lost income. In May 2020, Goldman Sachs reconsidered their optimistic pre-pandemic predictions, forecasting a 75 percent drop in live music revenue for 2020.[2] Two months later, Creative Arts Agency, arguably the entertainment industry's most prominent agency, let go of nearly 20 percent of its employees.[3] For creators themselves, empty venues from dive bars to stadiums have devastated incomes, communities, and morales.

As such, the music ecosystem is at a turning point. The decisions and solutions we form as a collective, today, could have longstanding impacts on the future of all individuals and entities who exist in this space. With creative disruption inevitably around the corner, don't we owe it to ourselves to

---

1 Daniel Sanchez, "Goldman Sachs Says Global Music Revenues Will Reach $131 Billion by 2030," *Digital Music News*, June 5, 2019.

2 Stuart Dredge, "Goldman Sachs: 'Global Music Revenue Will Drop by 25% in 2020'," *Music Ally*, May 18, 2020.

3 Wendy Lee, "Creative Artists Agency Cuts, Furloughs Nearly 20% of Its Staff Amid Pandemic," *Los Angeles Times*, July 28, 2020.

do our best to establish a system that works well—or at least better—for all of us?

Whether or not you realize it, the music ecosystem affects you, and me, and all of us every single day.

When you walk into a coffee shop and hear a pop song playing over loudspeakers, you are being sonically impacted by meticulous choices made by record executives and public rights organizations.

When you discover a new band on a Spotify algorithmic playlist, your behavioral data is being used to determine the trajectory of that group's potential.

When you go to see your favorite artist perform a show at an arena, you are joining a team of artistic devotees who are building a community—and a brand—around a given type of music, potentially shaping culture at large.

When you walk by a street performer on the subway and fleetingly consider whether you want to upload an Instagram story to shout them out to your small squadron of followers, you might just be putting that artist in front of the eyes of someone who could transform their musical journey.

To live in the world in our hyper-connected, digital age, is to engage with, be influenced by, and potentially impact the music ecosystem.

Furthermore, for those of us who work in the industry, music and the culture surrounding it plays an even more crucial role in our daily lives. Whether we're gigging around the city, reading trade publications to stay up to date on music technology trends, pitching press releases to publications for artists we manage, or scouting out songwriting talent at dive bars, we engage with the ecosystem as not just a soundtrack, but a lifestyle.

Like many listeners, music is, and always has been, the lens through which I see—and hear—the world. As a late '90s baby and product of the digital boom, I have personally belonged to and witnessed the origination and destruction of many musical phenomena. Whether I was using the dinner table as a drum or my hairbrush as a microphone, my parents always knew I loved music. At the ripe age of six, they introduced me to Hindustani vocal classical music, a tradition that centers on the concepts of improvisation and spontaneity as much as it does history and theory.

My eleven-year training in Hindustani music engendered in me an exploratory spirit that led me to a Sangeet Visharad, the Indian equivalent of a Bachelor of Music degree. Along the way, I developed affinities for other types of musical storytelling. From indie to alternative to pop to hip-hop to R&B to jazz to classical to electronic, I became a sonic sponge.

In my hometown of Los Angeles, I joined my first Western choir as a fifth-grader and was a member of my school's choral program for the entirety of my adolescence. I trained in a jazz choir throughout my junior and senior years of high school, adding Cole Porter and Ella Fitzgerald to my expanding list of musical idols. Through these ensembles, I performed and competed in some wondrous places—from The Hollywood

Bowl in Los Angeles to centuries-old cathedrals in Germany and Poland—introducing me to masterful musicians from all walks of life and artistic backgrounds. In high school, GarageBand and Logic became my haunts as I started writing my own music. I was honored to become a finalist in the Hollywood Songwriting Contest in mid-2016 in addition to completing my Hindustani curriculum.

At the same time, I was becoming increasingly fascinated with the business behind the music. I joined online music forums, learned how to track charts and make educated predictions as to how certain songs, albums, and artists would fare commercially, and I somehow managed to tailor my AP Economics term paper to music analysis (sorry, Mr. Nealis). I pored over industry magazines such as *Billboard* and *Hits Daily Double*, nerding out over creative and financial trends within the industry. When I went off to college, I was eager to turn my passion into a profession.

Once I reached New York University (NYU), I immersed myself fully in the music ecosystem. Crafting my own interdisciplinary concentration, which I titled Cultural Entrepreneurship, I explored the synthesis of social productivity and commercial development in the cultural industries.

Alongside my studies, I began my professional career, interning at some of the world's leading music companies, including Sony Music, Live Nation, and Roc Nation. I assisted executives at music festivals, composed music with fellow students as an artist-scholar, performed on tour in Japan with my a cappella choir, managed independent artists, moderated a panel interviewing leading music critics, and experienced dozens of live shows across genres, continents, and cultural spheres.

Today, I embrace this unique vantage point in each of my essays. From analyzing the nostalgic resurgence of vinyl sales to competing goals between tech-driven streaming services and independent artists to the ways in which we rely on music for emotional clarity during crises to many more topics, loud and soft, I aim to harness my multifaceted perspective and share it with you, hopefully providing clarity as the rain—and the basslines and the trap beats and the vocal runs—continues to pour.

As your guide on this journey, I will open out the questions I wish to ask. I will not rush to any easy conclusions, instead developing discussions drawing from many disciplines and my own personal and professional experiences. Having grown up in some of the most pivotal musical hubs in the world, surrounded by leaders across the field, I now understand that cultural movements and patterns have significant sociological consequences on the way people engage with music, reflecting broader notions of the evolving role of art in society. Now, I want to impart my many musings on this magic—and madness—to you.

I hope you will discover new wonders, sonic and beyond, if you decide to follow my lead.

MUSIC'S MYTHIC NIGHT

Dreams and Disillusionment at the Grammys

When I think of "music's biggest night," I think of a particularly peculiar night of my own. At nineteen years old, I attended the 2018 Grammys at Madison Square Garden.

The Grammys exist at the highest caliber of universally recognizable events. The annual awards show positions itself at the center of the musical realm, hailed as a celebration of the very best of creative innovation and a meeting place for all of the various players in the ecosystem to come together and appreciate the lifeblood of the entire operation: incredible art.

This premise might have been more palatable in years past, maybe even as recently as two years ago when I attended. Today, critics from all corners accuse the Grammys and its sixty-three-year-old parent company, the Recording Academy, of growing distant from the pulse of music's future. Artists and analysts wonder: is the academy struggling to propel an outdated business model and a myopic cultural perspective against a constantly evolving landscape?

Although today, it's easy to perceive the Grammys as an astounding but ailing relic of the recent past, I was once one of many believers. When I was a young teenager in the 2010s, watching the Grammys year after year in my living room felt like a staple of what it meant to be a music lover. I'd fantasize about what it might feel like to sit in the presence of so many artistic and entrepreneurial greats, hypothesizing about interpersonal link-ups that seemed unique to an event of such fanfare—*Sir Paul McCartney rubbing elbows with Madonna, oh my!*

How could I ever forget plopping down in front of my TV at age thirteen to be completely mesmerized by Lady Gaga's principal performance of "Born This Way," during which she hatched out of a translucent egg—or rather, *vessel,* as she insisted on calling it—as she swept the night's pop awards?

As an Arts & Entertainment Editor for my middle school's magazine, I conducted surveys asking the student body what their Grammy picks were as if I were polling a national election.

In 2016, months before graduating high school, I even threw a viewing party for the ceremony at my house, a celebratory avenue for me to cultivate my longstanding zeal for the music industry.

The iconic Grammy moments of my childhood, though distant in reality, felt intimate in my mind. I marveled in the myth that one night could encapsulate all that was important for people who cared about music.

On January 28, 2018, that distance dissipated. Hosted in New York City for the first time in fifteen years, the awards ceremony took place at Madison Square Garden, just blocks away from my NYU residence hall in Gramercy.

No, I'm not Elton John's recently discovered bastard child. No, I didn't take a bite out of some enormous trust fund to purchase a floor ticket. And no, I didn't have to blackmail anyone at the Recording Academy to score a seat. In fact, I was simply a member of Grammy U, a community of college students studying the music business who serve as student members of the Academy on campus and at industry events. Just weeks before that fateful Sunday, I received an email from the club offering the chance to volunteer as a seat filler at the show. I woke up at six o'clock in the morning to register, competing against hundreds as spots filled up within seconds. Although this opportunity ultimately came down to luck, for me, it represented the culmination of years of devotion.

Once I suited up in an outfit I purchased specifically for this night, self-injected a pep talk, and judiciously sprayed cologne on every surface and orifice of my body, I pondered just how bizarre it was that I was even able to partake in this experience while still in college. I had an essay due later that week, exams to prep for, emails to return, but none of it mattered that evening; I was about to fulfill a lifelong dream.

After a seemingly endless check-in process in the ballroom of The Hotel Pennsylvania, across the street from the Garden, security personnel laid out some ground rules to the collection of anxious seat fillers, dressed in our very best, shoulder-to-shoulder like sardines:

1. Don't speak unless you're spoken to.

2. Be camera-ready at all times.

3. Prepare for utter chaos during the commercial breaks.

As we waited for security to corral us into the arena, I small-talked with the restless cohort around me, some of whom were fellow Grammy U students, the others adults who had been given this opportunity by their employers. Another volunteer asked me who I worked for. When I told him I was still in school and working at the intern level, he raised an eyebrow and tilted his head, surprised by my age. As I feigned a calm and collected composure, I put the "fake it 'till you make it" idiom that had been drilled down into my head by teachers since I was a little kid to the test. Abandoning my impulse to chew my nails down to their cores, I sat and waited, absorbing the scene around me.

Before showtime, security escorted us through the arena's daunting web of passageways. Sleep-deprived agents sprinted by with haste, frazzled makeup artists popped in and out of waiting rooms, and the occasional entourage-adorned artist interrupted our line, prompting silence and eyes-faced-to-the-ground from members of our group. Each of us was given a green ribbon to pin on our suits and dresses, an indicator to artists and their teams that we were seat fillers and not invited guests (a critical distinction).

The Grammy U coordinators, in a pre-show frenzy, warned us that this situation would be a lot like musical chairs; they would direct us to fill seats as artists weaved in and out of the audience during commercial breaks. None of us should expect to stay in one place for the entire night.

Somehow, that's exactly what happened to me. Minutes before showtime, a coordinator ushered me into the arena and pointed to an empty chair. I scurried to my seat, inhaling the chaos around me, and within moments, Lana Del Rey flanked me to my right.

I pretended to be concerned with the neck of a guest in front of me, feigning nonchalance, as her bohemian, beige Gucci dress, ornamented with sequin-sheathed stars, brushed up against my shoulder.

"Hi. Would you mind switching with my publicist? I'd love to be on the aisle."

No, Lana Del Rey, how dare you ask me, a nineteen-year-old seat filler, to give up my seat on the aisle at the Grammys?

"Of course!"

As I shuffled past her, I rebelled against the rules and offered her a compliment.

"You look beautiful, by the way!

She gazed at me, thanking me with a lopsided smile. I'm fairly sure she even called me honey (assuming that I didn't hallucinate the whole damn thing).

Before I could take inventory of our exchange, the show commenced, and there I sat, nestled in the fourth row, giddy in all my just-post-adolescent glory. (If you happen to be on a nostalgia kick and want to rewatch the telecast, look out for me in the navy-blue suit and golden tie, sitting directly behind James Corden's strategically positioned parents, trying my absolute hardest to conceal the fact that I'm perpetually breaths away from entering cardiac arrest throughout the show.)

The telecast began with a breathtaking performance by Kendrick Lamar and U2. Their collaboration, "XXX," is a masterclass in harnessing pop culture as a political megaphone. A commentary on violent police protests, the spectacle culminated in the scene of fire-illuminated dancers crumbling to the ground following the sound of gunshots, mere feet in front of me.

To follow it up, as soon as Lord Lamar himself had plucked my last goosebump out of me, I noticed that Lady Gaga was testing out the microphone for her performance on a B-stage to my right, donning a pale-pink, angelic gown adorned with polar white feathers. To witness the wonders of two of my favorite recording artists alive, back to back, from such an intimate angle, after years of distant admiration, was nothing short of surreal.

Between the recorded moments of the telecast, commercial breaks of an entirely different nature ensued. While on camera, everyone in the audience remained poised and attentive, the second the house lights switched intensity during breaks, people spread like roaches in a prewar tenement. Attendees swapped seats, fled the room, and floated over to other sections of the arena to chat with friends and colleagues, uncloaking that the meticulously monitored telecast was but a grand performance. Beneath delusions of perfection lay panic.

Although no food was allowed in the arena, I snacked on pop-cultural confectionary that I won't soon forget, the kind that younger me would have dropped a jaw for: Pink sat two rows ahead of me, cozying up to her tutu-donning daughter. Cardi B and Offset held each other tight for the whole night, essentially sharing a seat. Sarah Silverman vaped periodically, in the general direction of DJ Khaled's son, Asahd, who inexplicably held a puppy in his lap. Jaden Smith popped over to at least a dozen artists to offer praise over the course of the night, all within my glorifying gaze.

Some of my observations, however, were more disheartening than awe-inspiring. I sat behind a country star who had just participated in a tribute for the victims of the 2017 Route 91 Music Festival shooting in Las Vegas. As soon as this artist returned to their seat after performing, I noticed that they were glued to Google, repeatedly refreshing United States trends. Seemingly, they were hoping to see their name on the list, seeking validation for their "selfless" act. Who knows—I might have done the same if I were in their position. But the juxtaposition of an apparently heartfelt tribute performance marking a devastating tragedy and this artist's craving for recognition was a stark reminder that when it comes to screen time, ego is a primary driver.

Other moments of the event were deeply comforting. At one point, I struck up a conversation with a woman next to me who told me she had worked the lighting for the event. The normalcy of our rapport made me realize that for every haloed mega-star in the room, there were teams of people who had helped make it happen, drawing upon a variety of different skill sets and lineages of passion, perhaps not unlike my own. I admired the synergy of an event that so many people had nurtured in ways big and small. I cherished that spirit of camaraderie.

Another stabilizing moment was Ben Platt's cover of "Somewhere" from *West Side Story*. Platt went to my high school, and I sang in the chamber choir with his equally brilliant younger brother. His ascension from a star on campus to a globally recognized artist has been a source of pride for me and my entire class. As his stunning vibrato stole the breath of everyone in the crowd, I paused to admire how far he'd come, reaping rewards he deeply deserved.

One of the standout "Grammy moments" of the night was Kesha's performance in support of the TIME'S UP movement. She sang her single, "Praying," an ode to recovery following her alleged sexual assault by Dr. Luke, a producer as tethered to controversy as he is the *Billboard* Hot 100 (for reference, back in September 2010, he was credited as a co-writer and co-producer on 40 percent of the chart's top ten).[4] Kesha fortified her protest anthem with a team of equally powerful women across generations and genres, from Cyndi Lauper to Andra Day to Julia Michaels.

According to a *Billboard* report written by Keith Caulfield, her "star-studded performance" marked "The most social moment of the GRAMMYs on Twitter … with forty-two thousand interactions."[5] The moment that stood out most

---

4 Chris Willman, "Dr. Luke: The Billboard Cover Story," *Billboard*, September 3, 2010.

5 "The Grammy Effect: Sales and On-Demand Streams of Music Performed at the 60th Grammy Awards Surge," Insights, Nielsen, updated February 5, 2018.

to the telecast's audience was also one of the most politically poignant, speaking to the kind of content viewers value in an era oversaturated with countless forms of entertainment. Despite the diminished cultural domination of television in the digital age, the Grammys continue to be a powerful driver of visibility and an opportunity to highlight important social causes.

The hours following the show were equally as mind-boggling as the telecast itself. Once I left the venue and turned on my phone, I received hordes of messages from, well, everyone I've exchanged words with in my life—and then some.

As text message after text message from unknown numbers poured in (one of them was from my childhood neighbor's mom whom I hadn't spoken to in about five years), my girlfriend sent me a video of our group of friends watching the show from her dorm room. They cheered me on with roars of disbelief as flashes of my face came in and out of frame in the background of the clip. By the intensity of their screams, you'd be fair to assume that I had received an award myself.

High on adrenaline and a dream fulfilled, I galloped my way back to my dorm on the freezing Midtown streets instead of taking the subway. I called my mom to relay all of the absurd things I had witnessed, exploring the possibility that sharing my observations with another would make it all feel more real (guess what: it didn't!).

Once I got back to my dorm room, I devoured an entire Joe's Pizza to myself. I couldn't coax myself to fall asleep until about three o'clock in the morning, fielding excited phone calls and Instagram comments from people from every phase of my life, just hours before my first class of the day on Monday morning.

* * *

For months following that night, being "the guy who went to the Grammys" became an identity that followed me. As a tour guide on NYU's campus, I regularly conveyed my experience as promotional fodder for New York City's wonders. Once, a prospective parent even told me she recognized me from her TV screen. I would have dismissed her comment as a creative attempt to secure her daughter a place at the school if she had been the only one to approach me. But every now and then, in dining halls, theaters, and classrooms, people would furrow their brows at me before asking me a question I learned to anticipate:

"Wait, have I seen you somewhere?"

This minuscule kernel of visibility was hysterical to me. All I did was sit down and observe, yet people treated me like I'd achieved some incredible feat. What must it feel like to be an actual performer, or any kind of active participant of the event, if merely attending is enough to garner such an intense reaction? Is TV really all that dead? It is certainly alive enough to have changed my life in some small way, and hey, I was just a green-ribboned seat filler for thirty-second increments, one night of one year.

As much as the Grammys continue to inspire some degree of awe in the eyes of the general public and, apparently, NYU's prospective applicants, those who work in music tend not to be so reverent.

At a boutique artist management company I interned for during my sophomore year, an influential boss told me how much she disdained the types of months-long campaigns—even lobbying—that were necessary to be considered for the Grammys, a trap one of the artists she worked with had fallen into. Some of my music business professors, all active practitioners in the field, noted to me that they had stopped attending the Grammys years ago since it no longer represented the best of the industry. I suppose its magical allure is aimed more at external audiences, not meant for those who are on the inside. At least, not anymore.

In recent years, the Recording Academy has battled more organizational controversy than ever in its history. In 2018, the year I attended, then CEO Neil Portnow ignited a media inferno when he urged female nominees to "step up" when asked why more women hadn't won televised awards. He soon resigned.[6]

A year and a half later, the new CEO, Deborah Dugan, mysteriously left the company before filing a forty-four-page complaint alleging "gender discrimination, sexual harassment and unequal pay on the part of the academy." The complaint also claims that the organization retaliated against Dugan after she raised concerns—in an email to a senior human resources executive—that the academy was operating under a "'boys'

---

6   Andrew Flanagan, "Grammy President Neil Portnow to Step Down in 2019," *NPR*, June 1, 2018.

club' mentality," according to *The Washington Post*.[7] Crucially, she also accused the institution of being corrupt, favoring the most connected artists and their teams as opposed to using quality as a metric.

Moreover, the Recording Academy has been shunned by heavyweight artists in the industry, such as Drake and Justin Bieber—both of whom are Grammy winners, mind you—for years.[8]

In 2016, alternative R&B artist Frank Ocean—also a Grammy winner himself—refrained from submitting his critically lauded album *Blonde* for consideration. "That institution certainly has nostalgic importance," he explains in a conversation with *Billboard*. "It just doesn't seem to be representing very well for people who come from where I come from, and hold down what I hold down." As a person of color, Ocean claims a responsibility to resist an "awarding system" and "nomination system" that he deems dated. "I'd rather this be my Colin Kaepernick moment for the Grammys than sit there in the audience."[9] The Grammys' reputation is stained by a years-long track record of nominating Black artists for flagship awards but ultimately only awarding them in culturally specific categories, a tacit form of segregation.

---

7   Bethonie Butler, "The Recording Academy Is Imploding the Week before the Grammys. Here's What We Know," *The Washington Post*, January 23, 2020.

8   Colin Stutz, "Drake Won't Be at the Grammy Awards," *Billboard*, January 30, 2017; Sam Moore, "Justin Bieber to Miss 2018 Grammys Ceremony despite Being Nominated," *NME*, January 26, 2018.

9   Colin Stutz, "Frank Ocean Explains His Decision to Sit Out 2017 Grammys," *Billboard*, November 15, 2016.

The Academy has also been critiqued for constricting its female nominees. In 2018, Lorde was conspicuously the only woman nominated for Album of the Year yet the only nominee not invited to perform a solo song at the ceremony.[10] A year later, Ariana Grande decided to forego attending the ceremony after producers inexplicably denied her the chance to perform the single she was promoting at the time.[11]

Many of the institution's transgressions have been under the immense scrutiny of a generation whose members are characterized by their inclination to critique the brands they consume—and hold them accountable. The numbers reflect the mutters: 2020 saw the ceremony's twelve-year-low in viewership.[12]

Evidently, the Grammys have a critical branding problem. Distancing oneself from the event has become more than just an act of subversion, but in fact, a marker of authenticity—even coolness—for many mainstream artists.

SZA spoke to *Pitchfork* after she left the 2018 Grammy award ceremony empty-handed despite being nominated for five awards. "I never looked at the internet [after the Grammys]. I never looked at anything anyone ever said," she insists. "Perhaps people place too much importance on the institution."[13]

---

10 Butler, *The Washington Post.*

11 Krystie Lee Yandoli, "Here's the Drama Between Ariana Grande and the Grammys," *Buzzfeed,* February 6, 2019.

12 John Koblin, "Grammy Awards Hit 12-Year Low in TV Viewers," *The New York Times,* January 27, 2020.

13 Braudie Blais-Billie and Jazz Monroe, "SZA on Ctrl: "I Didn't Even Fuck with My Own Album," *Pitchfork,* February 28, 2018.

Ironically, SZA's lack of support from the Grammys has fortified her 2017 album *CTRL's* cult status, potentially benefiting her far more from a marketing perspective than a win would have.

In February 2019, days after her spat with Grammy producers, Ariana Grande explained in an interview with radio host Zach Sang that few of her favorite artists have ever won Grammys. More often than not, she finds herself disagreeing with the Academy's choices as a fan. She has never used it as a yardstick to gauge quality.[14] At the event, she scored her first golden statue for 2018's *Sweetener*, despite not being present to collect her award. In the era of artists as autonomous brands with more power than ever to control the creation and distribution of their work, losing the support of the most streamed female artist of the moment did not bode well for the waning Academy.[15]

Some argue that we, as a society, have outgrown award shows altogether due to political and demographic evolutions. *Time* TV critic Judy Berman notes that "Awards shows are … suffering from the political polarization of the American public, as partisanship invades sectors of society that used to be essentially neutral ground and nurtures the vitriol with which conservatives … attack Hollywood types for their left-of-center views." Additionally, "Gen Z-ers aren't just streaming natives; they're devotees of social video platforms like YouTube and TikTok, whose homegrown stars (Lil Nas

---

14 Zach Sang, "Ariana Grande 'thank u, next' Interview," Zach Sang Show, uploaded on February 9, 2019, YouTube video, 1:23:36.

15 Noah Yoo, "Grammys 2019: Ariana Grande Wins First Grammy," *Pitchfork*, February 10, 2019.

X, Lilly Singh) only show up on the red carpet once they've crossed over to conventional fame," complicating the dynamic between traditional and new media.[16]

Music and technology journalist and researcher Cherie Hu, the owner of the popular newsletter and membership community *Water & Music*, further questions the fundamental premise of the award ceremony. "Genre categories in general do not adequately reflect the amazing cross-pollination of styles happening in music right now, especially from Black artists," she claims in a June 2020 tweet, since "Creativity refuses to be pigeonholed." Hu's assertion was a reaction to the Recording Academy's announcement that it would be retitling its "Urban Contemporary" category as "Progressive R&B," a decision met with collective eye rolls from critics who have been advocating for such a change fruitlessly for years. Twitter user @MacBoucher1 responded to Hu's tweet with a proposal to replace the traditional awards ceremony with a festival of artist appreciation, free of competition, a prospect Hu seemed to celebrate.[17]

But would people really tune into an artist appreciation ceremony? *Variety* Senior Music Editor Jem Aswad believes those hoping to dismantle the Recording Academy may be undervaluing the crux of its allure. "It's impossible to imagine music without Grammys. It's what you strive for. It's the Oscars. It's the Super Bowl. What if they took away the Super Bowl?" he wonders in a January 2020 *Spectrum News*

---

16 Judy Berman, "Award Shows Are Dying. Is That Such a Bad Thing?" *TIME*, January 16, 2020.

17 Cherie Hu (@CherieHu42), "This seems......... not better.," Twitter, June 10, 2020, 12:10 p.m.

report.[18] Perhaps, the attention of an audience is contingent on the high stakes that result from competition.

If a music industry devoid of the Grammys entirely is farfetched, significant reform of the ceremony is indubitably necessary. Even the new Recording Academy CEO Harvey Mason has acknowledged as much, promising to continue promoting institutional changes that he claims will push the Academy in the direction of greater transparency.[19]

When I attended the event, what became transparent to me was that the group of people in charge was not inherently better than anyone else, prone to the exact kind of behavioral kinks and chaotic disarray that we all are. Perhaps acknowledging this bias could be an asset for the Recording Academy. Instead of positioning the Grammys as "Music's Biggest Night" categorically, the Academy should acknowledge that its perspective stems from the perceptions of the specific group of people it is composed of, bringing along with them all their idiosyncratic preferences, agendas, and tastes.

What is outdated about the award show model is the notion that one institution can reflect universally applicable notions of quality. In the era of unprecedented consumer discovery, that suggestion is laughable at best and nefarious at worst.

---

18 Bianca Rae, "Variety Senior Music Editor Discusses Future of the Grammys," *Spectrum News 1*, January 25, 2020.

19 Jem Aswad, "Recording Academy Chief Harvey Mason Jr. on Social Change and What the 2021 Grammys Might Look Like," *Variety*, June 10, 2020.

The more the Grammys lean into what makes their perspective unique, as opposed to feigning universality, the more they can justify their continued existence. To do so would be truly transparent and would appeal to the expectations of a new generation while assuaging frustrations of generations past.

Doesn't it feel great when the Grammys "get it right"? When Esperanza Spalding won Best New Artist in 2011 over more predictable picks such as *Never Say Never* era Justin Bieber, the Grammys were able to generate exposure for a "thrilling, genuinely obscure talent," as described by Judy Berman.[20]

It was gratifying when Tyler, the Creator's mom joined him on stage during his first win in 2020 and yelled out a resonant "that's my baby," and even more so when he responded to an old tweet from 2011 written by a hater who cruelly predicted he would never win.[21]

In the cinematic realm, at the 2020 Oscars, South-Korean *Parasite*'s Best Picture win seemed to send much of the world into a state of celebration, indicating how much we rejoice when a piece of incredible art actually scores the recognition it deserves in spite of—or because of—its lack of conventionality.[22]

Critique as we may, there is a personal and societal victory in being affirmed by the dominant culture that an institution

---

20 Berman, *TIME*.

21 Callie Ahlgrim, "Tyler, the Creator Responded to Someone on Twitter Who Told Him He'd Never Win a Grammy 9 Years Ago," *Insider*, January 27, 2020.

22 Hannah Giorgis, "Parasite Won So Much More Than the Best Picture Oscar," *The Atlantic*, February 10, 2020.

epitomizes. Perhaps we can keep that joy alive but make it clearer who the principal arbiters of that culture are and how and why they are making some decisions over others, instead of accepting them as indisputable, mythic canon.

The role of institutions like the Grammys is that they provide context, a lens to filter through an abundance of content. And as much as institutions hoard power, they can use that very power to elevate the downtrodden. For a long time, we've rewarded them equally for doing both. Perhaps, we should push them to prioritize the latter.

As a Gen-Zer myself (barely, but proudly), I envision a Grammys that lifts the veil on the reality of who makes up its voting board, not just in press releases but during the telecast itself. I envision a Grammys that listens and learns, incorporating its audience into the conversation instead of treating them as distant spectators. I envision a Grammys that rewards artists for producing art in the first place, instead of reinforcing archaic standards that engender conformity and cutthroat competition.

Call me quixotic, but with the right kind of leadership and diverse perspectives fostering change, why shouldn't the show be able to recalibrate? Why couldn't it be more honest about what it is (and what, in reality, it has always been), and in doing so, revamp its business potential? According to a 2017 study from the American Marketing Association, "Generation Z expects brands to be transparent and authentic."[23] To

---

23 "Gen Zers Are Redefining Brand Loyalty," Blog, American Marketing Association Toronto, updated December 14, 2017.

achieve this end, the Grammys must redefine its fundamental principles. The same old will simply not be enough.

Sitting in that arena at nineteen was one of the most exhilarating experiences of my life, and equally, one of the most illuminating, a reality check into the logistical apparatuses that fuel the mainstream music industry and a peek behind the veneer of glamour and performativity that define such events on TV screens. Hopefully, the next time I attend, I'll be stepping into a more equitable, more transparent, but equally magical world. Maybe when that time comes, they will have done away with green ribbons. If we're lucky, they will have done away with genres too.

IDEALISTIC INELASTICITY

Bursting the Ticketing Bubble

How far would you be willing to go to witness Beyoncé belt "Halo" in person, Travis Scott electrify an arena with *ASTROWORLD*'s adrenaline-pumping anthems, or The Rolling Stones soar through a catalogue of their most iconic hits? What, rather, would you be willing to give up, to see your favorite artist live on stage?

The conclusion of the 2010s saw the live music industry in a state of economic bliss. In *Pollstar*'s 2019 end-of-year report, editor Andy Gensler is effusive, with good reason: "There is but one word to sum up the larger five-year industry trend … Growth."[24]

From 2015 to 2019, the average price of a concert ticket grew from $73.86 to $94.83 in North America and $78.30 to $96.17 internationally.[25] From a business standpoint, these notable

---

24 Andy Gensler, "2019 Business Analysis," *Pollstar*, December 16, 2019.
25 Ibid.

surges are promising indicators of unimpeachable prosperity for artists, managers, agents, and concert promoters alike. But while simply analyzing statistics might indicate that fans are willing to pay more and more for ticket sales, the industry should be wary of the long-term dissatisfaction listeners might associate with the increasingly consolidated and inaccessible live music apparatus.

The key element to the continued rise of mega-successful tours is, of course, fan commitment. If fans love an artist enough, there appears to be no perceptible limit to what they will contribute to catch them in person. Although "the average price of a ticket to the one hundred most popular tours in [North America] has almost quadrupled over the past two decades. … Fans of all types are paying more to see their favorite musicians," beyond just "the super wealthy who pay thousands of dollars to see the best acts from the front row," as analyzed by Lucas Shaw in a September 2019 *Bloomberg* article.[26]

Surely, my behavior has factored into this statistic. When Tame Impala's Kevin Parker made his way to Madison Square Garden during the summer before my senior year of college, my girlfriend and I shelled out hundreds of dollars to score floor tickets without extensive consideration. Since Parker only tours sporadically, we didn't treat our decision to splurge like just any other expense. There was little we wouldn't have done to experience the laser-laden, notoriously psychedelic stage show that our favorite artist was famed for putting on.

---

26 Lucas Shaw, "Concerts Are More Expensive Than Ever, and Fans Keep Paying Up," *Bloomberg*, September 10, 2019.

Just one pesky problem: his offerings on Ticketmaster were snatched up within seconds of being put up for public sale, perhaps by super-fans more eager to stare at a screen than us, but more likely because of the deviousness of stealthily positioned ticket scalpers and corporate pre-reservations. Reluctantly, like many downcast ticket-seekers, we resigned to the secondary market, spending weeks of our grocery budget on obscenely marked up general admission tickets from StubHub in an all-too-familiar, panic-ridden frenzy as prices hiked up by the half-hour until we clicked confirm.

With vacated wallets, we showed up hours before showtime on the night of the concert, eager to secure spots as close to the stage as possible. It was a worthy deal, but an ordeal nonetheless.

Concerts are more costly than ever, and apart from a privileged percentage of music fans who can flexibly allot discretionary income to buying tickets on a whim, "how much" is more than just a question of money. Instead, it entails a complex combination of time, energy, dedication, and tolerance of a system that increasingly caters to the mega-rich.

Endless growth can entail intangible costs. As the market becomes saturated with an abundance of increasingly expensive concerts, business proponents of live music risk alienating the types of fans who matter most in the long run.

Take Bex Paul, who, according to the aforementioned *Bloomberg* article, has seen Pink live on dozens of occasions since 2002, eleven times in 2019 alone, even though ticket prices for her shows have heightened rapidly. While Paul consistently arrives at venues hours before the shows start to snag the best spots, she is often overtaken by high-paying VIPs who harness money in lieu of organic fan support.[27] Is a dynamic that devalues diehard fandom truly sustainable?

These trends of growth disguise front rows filled with rich but oftentimes passive fans, as opposed to champions of a given artist's work with the capacity to enthusiastically belt out every word and direct positive energy back to the performer on stage.

During the summer before my junior year of college, I interned at Live Nation, the world's top concert promoter. The company, which owns Ticketmaster, competes in a ruthless duopoly with AEG, the owner of the AXS ticketing service. Over the course of a fast-paced and invaluably informative summer, I worked onsite at more than thirty concerts. Despite the company's understandable prioritization of its VIP clientele, it was the veritable fans who ultimately proved most valuable. These fans were the ones who returned year after year for the summer's flagship shows. These fans saved up for merchandise, splurged on liquid luck to elevate their nights, and became unsolicited ambassadors for the artists and the company by broadcasting their experiences on social media. While VIP clients were inconsistent in their level of commitment beyond their initial contribution, these true fans were generative before, during, and long after the shows themselves.

In January 2016, the New York attorney general's office conducted an in-depth analysis of the ticketing market,

---

27 Lucas Shaw, "Concerts Are More Expensive Than Ever, and Fans Keep Paying Up," *Bloomberg*, September 10, 2019.

finding that such fans face higher barriers to entry than ever. "The majority of tickets for popular concerts are diverted away from the general public," the study notes. "On average, only about 46 percent of tickets are reserved for the public. The remaining 54 percent of tickets are divided among two groups: holds (16 percent) and pre-sales (38 percent)."[28] Robotic scalpers and online pirates have certainly contributed to the corruption of the music market, but the primary ticketing industry itself has also played a hand in embittering its consumers by championing a business model that thrives on inaccessibility.

While we can at least partially attribute a rise in ticket prices to increased production value via technological advances—lest we forget Kanye West's tilted stage nor Taylor Swift's stadium-sized mechanical snake nor Lady Gaga's Born This Way Ball castle—it is the baffling amalgamation of service fees that induces the most frustration from would-be-giddy fans.[29]

Kristen Arnold is a close friend of mine from college who works in international development. She is, perhaps, one of the most excitable music fans I've ever met; her favorite artists are as dear to her as family. To hear her rave about the K-pop girl group BLACKPINK is to hear a child profess their love for Disneyland.

---

28   Eric T. Schneiderman, *Obstructed View: What's Blocking New Yorkers from Getting Tickets* (New York: Attorney General's Office, 2016), 11.

29   Steve Knopper, "How Kanye West Made His Saint Pablo Stage Fly," *Rolling Stone,* September 7, 2016; Zoe Weiner, "Taylor Swift's Snake—Whose Name Is Karyn, BTW—Stole the Show at the 2018 American Music Awards," *Glamour,* October 10, 2018; John Mitchell, "Lady Gaga's 'Born This Way Ball' Stage Biggest Ever Built to Tour," *MTV,* May 2, 2012.

In December 2019, on a crowded subway ride, she vented to me about her gripes with the ticketing apparatus. Hoping to buy tickets for Billie Eilish's headlining show at Madison Square Garden, she woke up before work, willing to wait for hours to grab tickets, only to be deterred by seemingly predetermined technical difficulties once they went on sale. Plus, "the fees were a third of the price of the ticket. Excuse me? Really?"

Kristen was forced to face a difficult, but relatable dilemma for any newly independent Gen Z-er: keep half of this month's paycheck, or engage in a once-in-a-lifetime experience she would never forget.

"I just miss the idea of concerts that you just go to spontaneously," she told me. "You could spend not too much money to see random artists you've never seen before. Now, you're only going to see people that you're willing to drop a whole lot of money on." The obstacles that envelope the search for concert tickets are ultimately "pushing away people that could become new fans."

Some artists have understood the urgency of tending to fan loyalty, making active efforts to mitigate some of the most pressing issues plaguing the ticketing experience. In February 2020, rock band Rage Against the Machine "set aside a tenth of the tickets at each venue of their upcoming tour to 'resell' themselves at a higher price, but still less than what scalpers are charging. The band then [gave] that extra money to charity rather than lining the pockets of ticket resellers," as analyzed by Josh Chesler of *Spin Magazine*.[30]

---

30   Josh Chesler, "Rage Against the Machine Raises $3 Million Combating Ticket Scalpers," *Spin*, February 16, 2020.

Other artists have ensured that tickets will be accessible to their true fans in the form of fan club exclusive pre-sales and direct-to-fan purchasing options. A slew of superstars have hopped on the popular promotional trend of selling out intimate shows at small venues to engage fans at accessible price points.

On a Zoom call several months after our first collaborative rant, Kristen recalls attending a one-off Halsey concert in May 2019 for just $17 at New York's beloved Webster Hall, which holds a capacity of under fifteen hundred people—far fewer than the twenty thousand or so that the alternative pop Grammy nominee typically draws in.[31] These tight-knit concerts loop fans into a once-in-a-lifetime experience with an unforgettable energy exchange, often impacting them far more than an arena show ever could. "What makes a good concert is how the fans interact with artists and how the artists interact with their crowd," Kristen insists. "Why not start making concerts more accessible to the people that actually listen to the music—your loyal fans—and *also* to attract new types of fans?"

After all, the victorious state of live music at the end of the decade proved ephemeral, a zenith preceding a drastic decline. On March 12, 2020, Live Nation paused tours internationally due to concerns surrounding the spread of coronavirus, a necessary step that bungled former predictions of the live music ecosystem's continued ascension.[32] Less than six months later,

---

31 Alternative Press Magazine, "Halsey Announces Intimate Era Shows, Fans Speculate Next Single," *Alternative Press Magazine,* May 2, 2019.

32 Dave Brooks, "Live Nation Planning to Pause Arena Tours Due to Coronavirus," *Billboard,* March 12, 2020.

Billboard reported that Live Nation's revenue had declined more than 98 percent year on year as a result of the pandemic shutdowns, with no clear rescue in the pipeline.[33]

Any reservations fans once had about attending live shows have likely been exacerbated by the devastation of the crisis. Even when a vaccine does arrive, each potential attendee will be marginally less likely to rush into the chance to submerge themselves in a live audience; as a result, fans will likely require grand incentives—or at the very least, logistical accommodation at a higher standard than the ticketing industry is notorious for—to make the decision to spend and attend.

Coronavirus has force-fed many industries the opportunity to restructure and rethink their fundamental operations, priorities, and business objectives; it behooves the live music world to seize theirs. Ticketing is the next facet of the music ecosystem that is overripe for structural disruption, its streak of reckless glory hampered by the times.

"I don't even want to go to concerts at all anymore," Kristen jokes with me after concluding her laundry list of grievances on ticketing, all of which I have heard reflected by other friends, including those who work in music. We should be wary of the seemingly inelastic demand for concert tickets. What appears like complete willingness to pay or do anything on paper might mask unquantifiable notions that pose long-term, structural consequences. If fan commitment is the factor

---

33 Glenn Peoples, "Live Nation Revenue Down 98% Due to Pandemic Shut Downs," *Billboard*, August 5, 2020.

that has driven substantial growth leading up to the virus, it is the one metric that we should try to nurture above all else as we prepare for a transformed landscape.

Beyond fan pressure, the unregulated concert industry is battling intensified legal scrutiny. In May 2020, US Senators Amy Klobuchar, Richard Blumenthal, and Cory Booker sent a letter "urging the Department of Justice to ensure that a vibrant and competitive live performance marketplace will exist after the coronavirus pandemic. ... When Americans are ready to go back to stadiums, theaters, and concert halls, they deserve a competitive marketplace that offers value, choice, and a variety of entertainment experiences." Live Nation and AEG's duopoly may, at last, be on the verge of being dismantled, or at the very least, held accountable: "we urge you to closely monitor these markets during and after this pandemic."[34]

For a long time, the numbers appeared promising and prosperous. But music is too mercurial for us to categorize it like just any other commodity. Overcommercializing the experience of live music might drain it of its singular essence, ultimately turning away the consumers that drive it.

Artists, and the teams supporting them, can boost brand affinity from fans by focusing on experiential quality instead of just monetary quantity, ultimately shaping a business model that is both sustainable and satisfactory for buyers and sellers alike. Shouldn't any business' top priority be the continued contentment of its primary customer base?

---

34 Jem Aswad, "Senators Klobuchar, Blumenthal, Booker Push Justice Department for Competitive Concert Ticket Prices," *Variety,* May 14, 2020.

The phenomenological experience of going to a concert for an artist one truly loves is what fuels the kind of lifetime value that is unique to music. Instead of chasing short-term rewards from fickle guests of honor, we should set up a system grounded in equity, one that is more receptive to paving pathways for diehard fans and casual music listeners alike to attend their dream concerts at price points that aren't padded with unreasonable fluff. If music ticketing is set up to privilege the fiercest fans, they are certain to come back for more, tour after tour, crisis after crisis.

DON'T CALL BLU DETIGER AN OVERNIGHT SUCCESS

Discipline and Detours in the Digital Age

"Oh my god. It got to a point where I wasn't sleeping at all. Really bad. I would DJ until four in the morning and then go to the library at, like, four-thirty."

Blu DeTiger and I are reminiscing on our first year at NYU. We met in an introductory writing seminar centered on musical subcultures, and yes, she was just as excruciatingly cool then as she is now. During roll call, her birth name rolled off of our teacher's tongue in such a syllabically satisfying manner that the rest of us post-pubescents silently understood she was bound for greatness. The majority of us were attempting, quite poorly, to feign external confidence as we barreled into the nebulous realm of attending a massive university in the world's cultural epicenter. But Blu, a New York native who grew up with artistic parents and her brother, Rex, just across the street from campus, was unfazed, her blonde mane framing blue-gray eyes that twinkled with long-cultivated self-possession.

After our class ended, I strolled back to my dorm to mingle with my floormates. Blu, on the other hand, rushed uptown to play an unpaid gig at New York Fashion Week: "I remember I had to storm out of class really fast, and I was all stressed out. I made my brother bring my stuff to the gig, so he met me there. ... I was just doing crazy shit like that all the time."

Blu has made her mark citywide as a bass-playing DJ, singer-songwriter, and producer famed for music that is genre-bending enough to fit into many jukeboxes across the soundscape. Her sound is funky and disco-driven to its core yet laced with pop perfection. Her visual aesthetic is retro and atmospheric; she's religiously committed to chromatic glitter, plunging bodysuits, and a blue streak in her hair that matches her signature blue Fender.

On "Vintage," an unreleased track she soon plans to unleash, she croons out a sleek chorus reminiscent of Foster the People's "Pumped Up Kicks" if it had been revamped for a rooftop party in Alphabet City. "I'm a vintage girl hanging with the flashback kids—I need a vintage boy for my outfit," she warns.

All of her tracks, each seemingly more refined than the last, are as NYC-friendly as a three o'clock in the morning cheese slice from Joe's Pizza or an orange—dare I say, "Tangerine"— colored sunset over the Hudson River.

Nearly four years, a couple more shared classes, and a series of run-ins at summer festivals and East Village bars past our first day of school, we are finally catching up over Zoom against silly virtual backdrops from coast to coast (she's covered up her New York abode with a blue-tinted shot of the Earth from space, and I've masked my childhood home in Los Angeles with a photo of a disco-ball-illuminated lounge at Joyface, my favorite bar in NYC and one of her frequent DJ joints). It's the spring of 2020, and I'm weeks away from snagging my Bachelor's degree; she's well on her way to stardom, rolling out singles from her debut project to 130,000 monthly Spotify listeners and (rapidly) counting (at the time of publication, that number has now multiplied to 1.1 million).[35] Time has flown fast, and somehow, we are both coming of age.

The tumultuous events of the past few months have rearranged any trajectories we thought we could map out for ourselves, one detour arising after another. The graduating Class of 2020 will forever be pitied for missed milestones, fumbled rites of passage, and generational disillusionment. Although Blu has been on a leave of absence from NYU's Clive Davis Institute of Recorded Music since her first opening gig for The Knocks in early 2019, her own kind of commencement—one that would have led into the dynamic, globe-trotting life of a solo artist with a fast-growing, wide-reaching, and well-solidified fanbase—has also been stunted.

"When all of it got canceled and postponed, I was so upset, almost to the point where I was, like, fuck, I'm gonna get depressed when I get home because—what am I gonna do?" she recalls. Initially set to go on tour in Europe with pop singer Fletcher and to continue a string of show dates accompanying indie idol Caroline Polachek, she returned home to shelter in her family's apartment in New York weeks earlier

---

35 Murray Stassen, "The Hottest Independent Artists in the World: Blu DeTiger, Calynn Green, Dirty Blond, Olive Amun & Sara Kays," *Music Business Worldwide,* May 29, 2020.

than expected as a result of the coronavirus pandemic. "It's weird because my whole life is performing."

In a serendipitous turn, the months Blu has spent in quarantine have unveiled her as prolific and adaptable. Just as global chaos was starting to ensue, Blu struck gold on TikTok, the corporate behemoth of a social networking app that has broken records as the most downloaded app in one quarter ever, surpassing two billion downloads in April 2020.[36] After beginning by posting short covers, boasting her unique talent on bass and reharmonizing over beloved artists from Meghan Thee Stallion to Dua Lipa to Gorillaz, she grew to become a fixture on TikTok's coveted, algorithmically driven #ForYouPage, attracting the attention of hundreds of thousands of users and even a handful of online celebrities.

In addition to riffing off of existing tracks, Blu has used the evolving platform to draw attention to her own discography and personal brand, regularly participating in virtual concerts and stay-at-home festivals, and even filming the music video for her aptly titled single, "Figure It Out," on her iPhone.

Blu has proven she needn't rely on production value, for she *is* the production value. Her streaming and social numbers across channels have more than doubled since she became labeled as "Tik-Tok famous," an honor most Gen-Zers are, either explicitly or secretly, deeply envious of.

By using her platform to leverage an existing artistic identity instead of crafting a new one based on her audience's

---

36 Paige Leskin, "TikTok Surpasses 2 Billion Downloads and Sets a Record for App Installs in a Single Quarter," *Business Insider,* April 30, 2020.

reaction, Blu differs from many of her peers who have attained success on TikTok. This is, perhaps, her strongest and most singular asset. When labels notice traction on a TikTok hit, their impulse is often to "attempt to transfer the momentum from the anarchic, rapid-fire, amateur world of the app to the highly controlled, slow-rolling, big-budget world of Top Forty radio—to transmute hypermodern online popularity into old-fashioned cultural ubiquity," as described by *Rolling Stone*'s Elias Leight in a February 2020 feature.[37]

To a generation that relies on instant gratification and an abundance of content, a single hit in the background of a viral video often fails to induce long-term fandom—if that artist's only claim to fame is that ephemeral moment. But Blu had already been equipping herself for longevity before her numbers soared.

With heightened fame has come heightened fanfare. Blu is now part of a select tier of artists whose daily lives are covered and curated by fan pages. @BlusWorldDomination on Instagram shares whimsical memes incorporating her name and likeness, vying for her affection and professing devotion in the comments section of each of her photos. "People always say, 'it's so cool, that you talk to your fans.' Why is that weird?" Blu wonders, smirking. She thrives when engaging with the people who value her gaze the most, even going as far as to send merchandise to those most dedicated and DMing them to chat, catch up, and exchange TV-show and music recommendations. "When's the world domination blu?" reads

---

37 Elias Leight, "Surprising No One, TikTok Is Driving a Lot of New-Artist Growth," *Rolling Stone,* February 28, 2020.

a predictable comment on Blu's post about a forthcoming livestream. I've been wondering the same damn thing.

It has been perplexing to witness Blu being pegged as some sort of overnight, digitally induced sensation. As her former classmate, I've long known of the countless nights and early mornings she's dedicated to pursuing her dream. By the age of seven, she had joined a lineage of artists including Blondie, Joan Jett, and Lady Gaga when she performed a Rolling Stones tribute at the iconic venue CBGB. Her new fans seem keen on imploring how she learned to master the bass during the pandemic-produced quarantine, unknowing of the lifelong discipline that has planted the seeds for such seemingly effortless virtuosity.

"I've literally been playing for fifteen years at this point, and I'm twenty-two," she insists. But the range of her fanbase represents an organic amalgamation of music lovers from across the globe, many of whom discovered her magnetism at live show opening acts or nights out at the club: "I've been touring forever and picking up random fans and followers since I started playing, and I think that it's really cool when people know me from different things ... everyone's coming together."

Perhaps, the notion of instant glory is a social myth. "What most people call overnight success is actually the market suddenly realizing the value of a great product or service that had been kept in obscurity for too long while its creators refused to give up," explains Luis E. Romero of *Forbes* in a 2016 op-ed.[38] Blu has been hustling to expand her footprint

---

38 Luis E. Romero, "Overnight Success Is a Myth -- Here Is Why," *Forbes*, August 8, 2016.

since long before the phrase "TikTok" referred to anything but the passing of time, or perhaps, a certain Ke$ha banger. As a young teenager, she embraced every gig that came her way, dominating Brooklyn warehouses, summer rooftop parties, and shady Manhattan bars that she shouldn't have been allowed into as a minor (some of them still owe her money, she notes, sporting a grin).

"I just always said yes to every opportunity," she tells me, "cause I knew that it would lead to the next thing." She stutters, and I get the sense that she's reflecting on blurry times: "I was only hanging out with thirty-year-old DJs ... it was very much, work, work, work. I tried to navigate the scene, and figure out what I wanted from it, and I was just doing everything. I met some really sketchy people." Blu emphasizes that she refrained from indulging in drinks or drugs during her sets, tiger eyes laser-focused on her craft.

As a young woman redefining the perception of a male-dominated instrument and music scene, Blu has had to overcome an ecosystem of naysayers who have been prone to discredit her. "I just wanted people to take me seriously, and I just wanted to get the next gig too. I wanted to be a professional. ... I think that also comes from being a girl ... and having to prove yourself extra hard," she reflects.

Despite practicing for hours in preparation for each slot she scored, she was determined to play it cool whenever she arrived at the venue. Like women across virtually every industry, Blu has faced a dual pressure to demonstrate her dedication and her skills while still exuding ease and remaining accessible, so as not to appear overbearing.

In her 2019 collection of essays, *Trick Mirror*, staff writer for *The New Yorker* Jia Tolentino breaks down society's constricting archetype of an ideal woman: "Everything about this woman has been preemptively controlled to the point that she can afford the impression of spontaneity."[39] Men are given space to thrive and publicly shed sweat along the way; women are expected to flourish, as if by a whim, without giving themselves ample credit for the personal grit that got them there. If they dare to defend the journeys that resulted in the final products, they risk the kind of unabashed scrutiny that is reserved for the objectified.

Blu is keen to shout out her supportive, creatively empowering parents and the mentorship of artists and musicians much older and well-versed than her; however, she is getting better at high fiving herself, attributing much of her success to the power of her own manifestation.

Although Blu could sell out most any bar gig today, she recalls many nights over the years when nobody would show up to her sets. "My brother," she tells me, "would pay for twenty tickets so his friends would come." The pair would announce themselves on guest lists that didn't exist, conjuring up an illusion of importance that they hoped would one day become the truth. "You personally care more about your project than anyone else does so you have to be the one to champion it and champion yourself," she advises, brimming with a sense of scope and wisdom that has been afforded by her practical education in the NYC nightlife circuit.

---

39   Jia Tolentino, *Trick Mirror: Reflections on Self-Delusion* (New York: Random House, 2019), 64.

On top of her deep-rooted self-confidence, Blu has developed a willingness to tackle unpredictability that fosters a spirit of resilience in such an intractable industry. In December 2019, her schedule was glaringly free, and she pondered the possibility of going back to school. Within days, she had lined up opening slots for global tours and mapped out opportunities until September. In March, when her entire plan for the year imploded, she recognized the potential in getting noticed on TikTok: "I would always write down in my notebook—I need a viral TikTok song, and it was a joke, but, it's not a joke, you know? I would tell my friends … any year, I'm just gonna become TikTok famous. I was kind of joking about it. But in the back of my head, I was like, no, I should do that."

Blu could, at least vaguely, envision the possibilities embedded in harnessing a trend to showcase her talent, a foresight that ultimately became fact because she struck at the right time. In a July 2020 interview with *Music Business Worldwide*, Roy LaManna, the founder of independent content distribution platform Vydia, raises concerns about a song-driven as opposed to an artist-driven culture: "… I hate to say it, but a lot of these TikTok hits, I mean, the artists could be an avatar—it wouldn't matter. That's why [we] are so focused on building the careers of real artists."[40] While any avatar or influencer could star in a TikTok, very few could replicate an artist fueled by years-long training, experience-driven street smarts, and a deeply-developed artistic brand. Blu's business intuition, packaged with relentless optimism, corroborates the otherwise idealistic notion that luck is hard work disguised.

---

40   Tim Ingham, "For a Lot of These TikTok Hits, the Artists Could Be an Avatar - It Wouldn't Matter." *Music Business Worldwide*, July 21, 2020.

On a daily basis, Blu is sent videos of fans attempting her infectious basslines and pleas for advice on her favorite audio equipment. "That stuff literally makes me want to cry, since, from when I started, that was always my thing. … I want to inspire young girls," she notes. "It kind of sounds stupid," she qualifies, as if by training. "But fuck. This is dope."

Leaning into her webcam, she lets me in on an exciting development: one of the most sought-after producers on the planet recently recruited her to play bass on a highly anticipated, *Billboard*-Hot-100 tailored pop record. He became besotted with the idea of working with Blu when his young daughter, a musician, saw one of her videos on TikTok, and approached him with a request: "Dad, I want to learn how to play the bass."

In a year like 2020, Blu's streak of successes seems at odds with a cultural climate that is conducive to downfall, not ascension. But the fact that her rise has been the result of her making the most out of an awful situation does not counteract the pain associated with that situation. For her, and for me, too, this is still a time of profound mourning.

While virtual shows have become the new normal, it is harrowing to consider the losses that will continue to confront the New York music and nightlife scenes as a result of the economic shutdown and a collective anxiety about gathering, the lifeblood of the live music ecosystem. Our playground for our most formative years—the sandbox of our youth—has been stripped bare, not predicted to fully recover until we will be in decidedly different phases of our lives, less eager and less encouraged to explore.

"The really crazy part," Blu worries, "is that no one knows when it's gonna go back to normal. … I just turned twenty-two, and this is the time to have fun, and go out, and experience New York." After years of hard work, it seems Blu was more than eager to play, to indulge in the rewards of her years-long grind at last and to revel in her accomplishments before entering an uncertain future. Like us college seniors, Blu is learning how to "Figure It Out" in a world that has been fundamentally reshaped. For now, TikTok domination, and healthy doses of nostalgia, will have to do.

As we wrap up our Zoom call, weeks before virtual graduation, we reflect on the final Saturday of February, the last night both of us had a chance to go out in NYC before the national shutdown. Blu was DJing a set on the top floor of the PUBLIC Hotel, a glamorous staple on the Lower East Side, and I was in the audience. My friends and I dressed up in our brightest bombers, all of our throats coated in excessive champagne, many of our eyelashes doused in glitter. Blu was wearing a multicolored long sleeve, framed by the freedom tower's silhouette looming above us through floor to ceiling windows. High on melodic and rhythmic dopamine, we bathed in the glory of a performer in her prime, a champion dominating her home court.

With her Fender in hand, Blu electrified the room of socialites and NYU stragglers alike, gifting us a night of unfettered euphoria. Who knows if or when that specific dance floor will ever open again? What's certain is that the ethos of that atmosphere lives on inside of Blu, strengthened by every hour she spends honing her craft, showcased by every unpredictable opportunity she tackles, without pause.

THE SPOTIFY DILEMMA

Music's Messiest Divorce

If you pause your Discover Weekly playlist for a quick moment, your ears might register a distant sound. Hear that sizzle? Many music lovers have beef with Spotify. Perhaps, I ought to have some too.

Spotify has garnered hordes of supporters across the musical stratosphere. With a user base surpassing 138 million paid subscribers—myself included—as of the second quarter of 2020, the publicly-traded company has secured its place at the helm of the audio streaming frontier.[41] Following a start to the millennium riddled with piracy, inaction, and the demise of archaic music revenue streams, Spotify has become an emblem of the music industry's reinvigorated potential for innovation.

One of Spotify's most enticing attributes is its unmistakable and ubiquitous brand identity, evoking notions of evergreen invention to the consumers who encounter its countenance.

---

41 "Spotify's Premium Subscribers 2015-2020," Music, Statista, updated August 21, 2020.

As a sophomore in college, I once published a defense of the platform in an NYU magazine when it turned a profit for the first time in April 2018, revering it as my beloved digital scrapbook, "black and green like an enigmatic grotto."[42]

Beyond proponents of the platform like myself, Spotify has collected a chorus of doubters. Before its infamous launch on the stock market, some music industry heavyweights chose to withhold their music from the platform due to what they deemed an unfair compensation model. Spotify, like its competitors in the streaming space, abides by what is known as a "pro rata" payment system, compensating rights holders' royalties based on the proportion of total songs streamed that an artist's streams make up, as opposed to a fixed price per song or album.[43]

In 2013, Thom Yorke and Nigel Godrich of Radiohead removed their music from the platform, deriding these low royalty rates.[44] A year later, in an essay published in *The Wall Street Journal*, Taylor Swift famously stood up for independent artists much less successful than herself by opting to withhold her catalogue from the streaming service entirely: "Music is art, and art is important and rare. Important, rare things are valuable. Valuable things should be paid for."[45]

---

42 Saransh Desai-Chowdhry, "In Defense of Music Streaming: How Spotify Helped Me Grieve When I Didn't Think I Deserved To," *The Tab NYU*, April 6, 2018.

43 Tim Ingham, "Should Spotify Change the Way It Pays Artists?" *Rolling Stone*, December 7, 2018.

44 Music Business Worldwide, "Thom Yorke Slams Spotify as Albums Are Removed," *Music Business Worldwide*, July 14, 2013.

45 Taylor Swift, "For Taylor Swift, the Future of Music Is a Love Story," *The Wall Street Journal*, July 7, 2014.

In October 2015, multi-instrumentalist and singer-songwriter Joanna Newsom notoriously labeled Spotify "the banana of the music industry," criticizing it for being a "cynical and musician-hating system."

"The business is built from the ground up as a way to circumvent the idea of paying their artists," Newsom told *The Los Angeles Times*. "I've walked out of grocery stores because I can tell that there's a banana over-ripening that's fallen under the produce bins. ... It's brown and gives off this gas. I can smell it walking in the door. ... It just gives off a fume. You can just smell that something's wrong with it."[46]

Beyond sizzles and smells, contentious debates surrounding Spotify continue to sprout up now that mainstream music streaming services no longer have to justify the very premise of their existence as they were once forced to. Wikipedia aggregator Wikiwand has dedicated an entire page to "Criticism of Spotify," including concerns centered on the privacy and security of users' listening data and personal information.[47]

Liz Pelly is one of the captains of the crusade. An award-winning critic at *The Baffler*, a political and cultural journal based in New York City, Pelly is fiercely concerned with defining and dissecting the digital platform economy and its impact on the music ecosystem. Specifically, she strives to unearth the underlying agendas that global corporations—namely heavily-funded,

---

46 Randall Roberts, "Q&A: Joanna Newsom Calls Spotify 'a Villainous Cabal' and 'a Garbage System,'" *Los Angeles Times,* October 18, 2015.

47 "Criticism of Spotify," Wikipedia, Wikiwand, accessed October 14, 2020.

technologically-oriented startups like Spotify—are prone to obfuscating as the music industry rebuilds itself.[48]

Pelly has targeted Spotify in several polemics as a contributing editor and in even more talking points within conferences and classrooms, including one of my own. During the first semester of my senior year in the fall of 2019, Pelly visited my cultural criticism class, encouraging me and my cohort of budding writers to understand the ways in which the lofty promise of Spotify conceals its biggest offenses. Our sixth-floor classroom's roundtable was dimly lit, the muffled evening cacophony on the intersection of Broadway and Washington Place underscoring our hushed discussion. As Pelly spoke, penetrative blue eyes highlighted by pitch-black eye makeup suited for war, her dedication to the subject was infectious. We grasped onto her every word as if she were briefing us on intelligence in the Situation Room.

In "The Problem with Muzak," a December 2017 article that has now become a cornerstone of her initiative, Pelly seeks to enlighten those "who have perhaps fooled themselves into trusting that this exploitative model will 'save the music industry'." She derides the hegemonic power of an institution that claims to promote music discovery while, in actuality, discouraging active listening.

Instead of facilitating disruptive artmaking, she says, Spotify reinforces the hyper-quantifiable commercial landscape's control over the artform of music. By prioritizing algorithmic curation and allowing brands to stealthily buy their way onto

---

48   "About," Liz Pelly, accessed October 14, 2020.

user-facing playlists, Spotify engenders a culture of passive consumption and creation in which users are decreasingly inclined to curate their own soundscapes, anything but a true music lover's ally.

Spotify is not, and never has been, artist-driven, despite finally—and hardly—becoming profitable. Pelly insists the platform's "obsession with mood and activity-based playlists has contributed to all music becoming more like 'Muzak,' a brand that created, programmed and licensed songs for retail stores throughout the twentieth century." Using this historical misstep as persuasive ammunition, she mobilizes her readers to confront the fact that "more gross revenue in the music industry does not in any way translate to an industry that is healthier or more sustainable for the majority of artists."

Pelly contends with these issues on a deeply personal level. Her background as a volunteer within community arts spaces reveals itself in her proclivity to stand up for the most marginalized arbiters of music culture: "These streaming services are literally the only option for a music career nowadays," notes Pelly's interview subject Greg Saunier, the drummer from Deerhoof, in her aforementioned piece in *The Baffler*.

How could we possibly position a framework that reduces all songs, great and grotesque alike, to mere "emotional wallpaper" as the only feasible route for artists to succeed in the digital age?[49]

On some level, I'd always believed—or at least wanted to believe—that Spotify is a symbiotic member of the music

---

49 Liz Pelly, "The Problem with Muzak," *The Baffler*, December 1, 2017.

ecosystem and not its antagonist. But if it does, like Pelly and her peers claim, threaten the very existence and sustainability of independent artists and organizations without the commercial prowess to combat a company of its magnitude, it appears to be more parasitic for the music ecosystem than mutualistic.

"Be an active listener," Pelly insisted, as she bid us farewell, the sun having long evaded the view from our window. "Have a *real* connection with music."

Pelly's critique lingered with me, heightened by bubbling discontent across the ecosystem. I pondered my own one hundred plus track playlists filled with far more songs that the algorithm serviced to me than those I handpicked. What did it mean that these soundtracks of my life—the colors and hues of my daily runs, late-night study sessions, and hurried walks to class—were so tailored to my narrative yet so devoid of the original context of each individual artist's vision?

Still, my ears resisted. Was she rushing to place the structural blame on a subset of a machine instead of blaming the broader conditions that produced it? Are Spotify's innovations truly extricable from the conversation? What about the fact that piracy was a pressing parasite that Spotify rectified by organizing a profitable, if unequal and imperfect, streaming infrastructure?

Spotify is emphatically not the first institution to commercialize the music experience by providing an illusion of choice to music fans. Radio stations and record labels have been doing it for years. Hey, back in the days of European monarchy, leaders of empires dictated which music pervaded the soundscape and which didn't.

What about the fact that "listening diversity," a metric that gauges users' propensity to discover new artists, has risen on Spotify by 40 percent per year according to an October 2018 press release, a heartening trend that may not have been tractable without the Spotify apparatus?[50] What of the musical exploration that Spotify renders accessible, which can gift us the guitar-coated dirge that we need to cope with the loss of a loved one, the motivational up-tempo we need before a daunting workout, or the pulsating pop bop we need to digest the saccharine syrup of a lustful romance?

If anything, isn't Spotify leveling the playing field more than those former institutions ever did?

Perhaps it is foolish to deem Spotify's structural offenses permissible, in the name of—what? Personal convenience? My emotional reliance on the clichés of the soundscape? Being conditioned to dedicate myself to a digitally-propelled-capitalistic-system that I've essentially been enveloped in since birth?

Yet I'd be a liar if I said my highly-listenable, earworm-adorned "Spotify Wrapped" end-of-year playlist wasn't an annual highlight of my December, self-indulgent, undeniably pleasurable, riddled with "Indietronica," and extremely easy for me to swallow.

I was surprised to discover that an employee within the operation itself would further dismantle my defense of the platform. "I'm just not sure if music streaming can be the model moving

---

50 "Celebrating a Decade of Discovery on Spotify," Newsroom, Spotify, updated October 10, 2018.

forward," notes my good friend, former colleague, and NYU Stern alum Nick DeMasi, who works as a Data Scientist at Spotify while moonlighting as an artist manager.

When we waxed analytical on FaceTime, deconstructing critiques of a company we'd both cosigned in our own ways, I certainly didn't expect him to empathize with the mob that was maligning his employer.

"There are three primary stakeholders. ... The checklist is always going to be, okay, how is this going to affect our subscriptions? How is it going to affect our relationship with our labels? And then, how is it going to affect the actual artists that are on the platform?" he says. "I don't think that Spotify is ever really making decisions that are for the best interest of the artists and the artists first."

Perhaps, Spotify's listener-first, artist-last approach is what has led me to absolve it of its shortcomings for so long. I benefit from being a member of the primary stakeholder class, the target audience for branding spectacles. Evidently, their courting efforts prove effective.

Spotify deemphasizes years of invisible labor from legions of artists in pursuit of my monthly $9.99, and, for years, I've even outwardly championed them as an unsolicited ambassador.

Dispelling my expectations even more, DeMasi reiterates Pelly's critique that Spotify's push toward passivity has harmed listeners just as much as artists. In turn, a pervasively passive listening culture fosters even more passive music creation, harming artists on yet another level in a seemingly endless cycle. Such a culture is certainly beneficial for the owners of an application who want to drive as much usage—passive or otherwise—on the platform as they possibly can.

Here lies the crux of the issue: for Spotify, music is a means to an end, a mere vessel to promote its broader platform, which is ultimately a technology service, not unlike any other oft-critiqued corporate giant.

DeMasi wields a personally meaningful vantage point as both an employee of Spotify and the manager of Juletta and Ishan, two rising independent artists whom I formerly helped him develop in the early stages of their career: "Music [has become] just the marketing for the artists. The goal of artists is not to create music. It's to create music so they can accrue scale. And *then,* they'll be able to make money."

This reality is disparate from one of Spotify's most public selling points, the notion that it gives far more artists opportunities to embrace their individuality and still succeed.[51] While Spotify is undeniably a tool for more artists to generate visibility for their unique brands and to reach audiences beyond their local communities more than ever before, it is unclear if this model is actually benefiting their ability to sustain their livelihoods. According to a 2019 *Pitchfork* article written by senior staff writer Marc Hogan, a survey from the *Music Industry Research Association* indicated that only 28 percent of respondents claimed to make any money

---

51 "We're Closing the Upload Beta Program. Here's What Artists Need to Know," Artists, Spotify, updated July 1, 2019.

at all from streaming royalties over the course of 2017, the median amount hitting just $100.[52]

On an internal level, Spotify now perceives much of the music industry as somewhat of a regular opponent. By positioning itself as an "audio-first" platform, with an intensified focus on investing in podcasts, it is diversifying to amass leverage over the music industry.[53] This shift is what has turned the weird marriage between the worlds of music and technology into what appears to be the unfolding of a messy divorce, lawyers and negotiations aplenty.

"Before, Spotify needed the labels because they needed the music. They needed the users," DeMasi explains. "But Spotify has enough users and cultural capital to continue on its own. And now the thing that's hindering them *is* the catalogue and the labels."

Spotify's critics have exposed disheartening realities to me, but I maintain my conviction that one institution cannot be subject to all the blame for propelling a business agenda that may be at odds with creative freedom. When we critique Spotify, we are not diagnosing a new problem as much as we are tracing the newest iteration of a systemic issue: art and commerce rarely, if ever, integrate without casualties.

If those of us within the music ecosystem are going to truly confront Spotify's threats to the prosperity we once

---

52 Marc Hogan, "The Record Industry Expects a Windfall. Where Will the Money Go?" *Pitchfork,* May 30, 2019.

53 "Audio-First," Newsroom, Spotify, updated February 6, 2019.

credited it for producing, we must equally acknowledge our own complicity. Many of Spotify's offenses run parallel to its competitors and other players in the industry, from labels to management companies to publishers. Spotify may be a technology company, but that does not justify a binary analysis on our part; perhaps, we can simultaneously recognize its merits while still holding it—and ourselves—accountable.

For one, listeners, like myself, can foster incremental change by reevaluating our listening habits and the type of immediate access to music we now feel entitled to. "Fans need to make a decision about who it is that they're going to support," insists DeMasi. Pre-Spotify, we perhaps didn't have enough artists to choose from. Now that we're faced with an abundance of artists, we are rarely driven to commit to any one of them with the intensity they require to survive and thrive as musicians. Unfortunately, Spotify benefits from concealing this truth, using its data-driven prowess to encourage our restless consumption tendencies. As Spotify the product grows stronger, it renders each individual artist increasingly reliant on it; our defiant commitment to specific artists can offset this shift.

DeMasi himself listens to Bandcamp in an attempt to approach music more actively and to fairly compensate his favorite artists. If someone on Spotify's payroll can resist the urge to blindly glorify it, I suppose the rest of us can too.

Bandcamp, heralded by some as the "anti-Spotify," allows artists and labels to upload music directly, independently control pricing points, and offer merchandise and extras to fans on their platform.[54] In September 2020, Stuart Dredge of *Music Ally* notes that the service's monthly sales are up 122 percent year-on-year: "In the past year, fans have bought 5 million digital albums, 2 million tracks, 1 million vinyl albums, 600 thousand CDs, 300 thousand cassettes and 250 thousand t-shirts from Bandcamp ... with more than 40 percent of buyers paying more than the asking price of items."[55]

In an interview with *Pitchfork*, digital music executive Vicki Nauman forecasts to Marc Hogan that the future of music will entail fragmented streaming services that appeal to subcultural artists and fans instead of the one-size-fits-all platforms that thrive today: "Market segmentation is next," since "Music is inherently tribal, and there are underserved fans waiting in the wings."[56] There is endless potential in the specialized activation of music listening, an imminent infrastructure that can continue to foster spaces for musical discovery without flattening the artists who fuel it. There is endless potential in any paradigms that champion the cultural agents that craft the music itself.

Ideally, the best aspects of music streaming should persist. Back in 2015, even Joanna Newsom followed up her fruit-focused accusation with a "wish" that "there was a way to provide the service they provide and have nobody lose, nobody be victimized by that."[57]

---

54 "What Pricing Performs Best?" Selling FAQ, Bandcamp Help Center, accessed October 14, 2020.

55 Stuart Dredge, "Bandcamp's Monthly Sales Are up by 122% Year-on-Year," *Music Ally,* September 23, 2020.

56 Hogan, *Pitchfork.*

57 Roberts, *Los Angeles Times.*

I still believe, as I outlined in my 2018 article, that music streaming's best asset is its potential for unbounded user search, the opportunity for me, or anyone else, "to discover my 'sad' or my 'frustrated' or my 'motivated' or my 'dance' or my 'in love' in the form of alien art—with just a few swipes on a screen." I still believe in streaming's "capacity to make the world smaller, to render an individual less alone, less repressed, less uninspired than square one."[58] I wonder if all of these capacities can exist, just in a framework that sees music as the bloodstream and not the IV.

As stakeholder number one, I am Spotify's guest of honor. As a proponent of music and the culture that surrounds it, I am also one of its foes. Understanding myself as a child of divorce helps me understand my equivocal stance. I can revere Spotify for what it provides me without neglecting how it puts the music ecosystem at stake.

Beef is difficult to swallow, especially if uncooked, though I wonder if such discomfort is crucial for our teeth and for our thoughts. Are we willing to take a bite?

---

58 Desai-Chowdhry, *The Tab NYU*.

MOURNING MY RECORD STORES

The Lineage of the Local Music Economy

"It's as if musicians were suddenly, like the new wave of farmers, able to grow smaller quantities of more interesting crops and find reasonably profitable markets for them ... the equivalent of farmers' markets, places that customers love not only for the product but for the experience ..."

—BILL MCKIBBEN IN *DEEP ECONOMY*[59]

If Spotify is a supermarket, a local record store is a farmer's market. Here, you may not find every fruit under the sun, but you might just happen upon the juiciest white peach you've ever eaten. You'll soon forget the breadth of hapless fruit from the supermarket, but you'll think about that extra special peach every day for the rest of your life.

Across the street from me lies the remnants of a local record store. It's the focal point of the view from my bedroom

---

59   Bill McKibben, *Deep Economy* (New York: St. Martin's Press, 2007), 167.

window, visible between the flimsy bars of my charred fire escape. "Rotten Island Records," its signpost reads, atop a call-to-action conveyed by chalk: "Buy. Sell. Trade."

Each morning as I walk by its boarded-up windows, masked, on my way to grab a bagel from the bodega it neighbors, I can't help but silently mourn the records of Rotten Island. Just a few months ago, they were ripe, ready to be cared for and consumed. Now, halfway through the strangest summer of my life, they are riddled with dust, separated from the mainland by a graffitied garage, stripped of sunlight, out of sight.

Now that the coronavirus pandemic has relegated me to the inside of my Bushwick apartment, I often wonder if I hallucinated the entire summer of 2019. Back then, I stormed a concert a week, a dance club a weekend, and a record store a day. Back then, vinyl sales were miraculously growing by 12.9 percent every six months, as per the Recording Industry Association of America's 2019 mid-year report.[60] Back then, the only stable factor in the music industry—and my collegiate life—was the certainty of growth. My relationship with music had never been so vibrant nor vital as it was during that formative period. I often wonder if that dynamic—and the thriving ecosystem it belonged to—will ever replenish itself.

The summer of 2019 succeeded the most difficult semester of my college career. Spring saw me stumble my way through a Pulitzer-prize-winner instructed fiction master class that equipped me with as much imposter syndrome as it did

---

60 Elias Leight, "Vinyl Is Poised to Outsell CDs for the First Time Since 1986," *Rolling Stone*, September 6, 2019.

literary prowess, alongside a twenty-five-hour-a-week, suit-and-tie demanding, stye producing Midtown Manhattan internship. As such, the start of New York's sunniest seasons that year served as a necessary sigh of relief. For the first time in a long time, I stopped rushing to keep up with myself around the clock. A huge part of that process was learning to engage with music on a different level than I was accustomed to: locally.

Some people grow up listening to records, visiting local music shops as a familial pastime. I, however, first claimed a music listening experience of my own on a gray and white SanDisk Sansa m200 that I received for my seventh birthday before graduating to a series of iPods I inherited from my sister. From being corrupted by a LimeWire addiction to ultimately being rescued by the interactive allure of the iTunes store (and some generous gift cards from family and friends), my coming of age has directly paralleled the dominating digitization of the musical landscape. My teens spanned everything from the dramatic death of the CD-ROM to the much-needed and much-debated monetization of the music streaming model.

Exceptions to my immersion in the digital domain were seldom. Sure, in tenth grade, my girlfriend and I spent a Sunday at Amoeba Records in Hollywood, filtering through stacks of records we didn't recognize and taking home a couple of CDs so we could read through the liner notes. However, since our parents dropped us off (we were fifteen), and since it took three-quarters of an hour to reach the hotspot (typical LA traffic), that visit felt a lot more like a field trip to a music history museum or a souvenir shopping spree than a cornerstone of our engagement with music.

For much of college, record stores continued to feel like relics of the past. In the heart of the semester that challenged me more than any other, however, I was given an opportunity to shift directions. On a late night in my dorm's dimly lit study room, I received an email to interview to become NYC's College & Lifestyle Marketing Representative for The Orchard, an aggregate distributor of independent artists and labels that was acquired by Sony Music in 2017.

While I was thrilled by the opportunity to take on a role at a company I'd admired (and applied to) for years, I knew this decision would be consequential. The junior summer of college can often greatly influence one's career trajectory, and I had always envisioned myself becoming more and more digitally involved, because, why wouldn't I? Wasn't digital the future—and the here and now—of music and all of its adjacent industries? I knew that I would be stepping out of my comfort zone by pivoting to an equal focus on the physical side of things.

But when else would I be able to get paid to promote at record stores, generate buzz for artists on campus, and host parties for my friends? When else would I be able to learn about the music industry from the ground up? Although it wasn't exactly what I had expected to be doing, this role felt uniquely tailored to this specific phase of my life. Warding off post-college regrets, I said yes to the unknown.

Being a College Marketing Rep at a music company is, in some ways, a rite of passage. In exchange for being a company's eyes and ears to target the elusive and impressionable college demographic, reps across the music industry are able to launch well-connected and experienced careers in music if they excel at the role. Some of my biggest inspirations in the music industry were once marketing reps during their college years, a chapter of their personal histories they'd fondly recollect during presentations in my classes and internships.

David Wander, the Chief Digital Officer of Jay-Z's Roc Nation, once told me during a lunch and learn when I interned at the company that being a rep for Universal Music Group is what jump-started his career and gave him the tools to learn how to succeed in the music business. Although Wander began as a rep back in 2007, twelve years before my start date, our job function was essentially the same. We were both tasked with promoting physically at record stores, putting up posters, handing out promotional materials, and galvanizing our personalities and networks to generate excitement around music in our local markets.

The simple notion that, as much as technology may evolve and change, some things do in fact stay the same over time is deeply reassuring in an industry that can never seem to stay in place. I was eager to join a lineage that had shaped many of the trailblazers I most admired.

The first day my team sent me out to promote at record stores, my undeniable excitement was muffled by a layer of nascent nausea. Sure, I'd held numerous positions in music before, but this was a whole different dance floor. The prospect of walking into physical stores and asking shopkeepers face-to-face if I could promote there was an interpersonal challenge no amount of data analysis or artist development expertise could help me overcome.

"Record store guys can be a little … grumpy," warned my boss, Allison Ullrich Kaiser, before my first expedition. Her portent equipped me to expect the worst, conjuring up anxiety reminiscent of a middle school lunchroom on the first day of school. Briefly, I envied my friends in suits doing data entry in high rise Midtown cubicles. What was I thinking taking a job like *this*?

The first record store I ventured into was Generation Records, a punk and metal leaning fixture on Greenwich Village's fabled MacDougal Street, just steps away from NYU's campus. My assigned task was to put up posters for three bands and leave Frank Iero branded sunglasses behind the counter to commemorate the release of his new record. Before I approached the tattooed, half-shaved-headed man behind the cash register, I dilly-dallied, feigning interest in the stacks of new records by the front of the store as if I were just another curious customer. Eventually, after more preparatory gulps than I can responsibly recall, I approached him and introduced myself, cosplaying confidence.

To my surprise, he was receptive to my query, not particularly effusive, but certainly not unapproachable in the manner I had expected.

Some of the other record store owners I encountered as I began my journey exceeded baseline politeness. At the neon-themed Halcyon Shop in Williamsburg by the East River, I struck up a conversation in French with a whimsical store owner who was originally from Montreal. At Village Music World on Greenwich Village's Bleecker Street, James and

Jamal welcomed me into their narrow entryway with warm smiles and helping hands adorned with skull rings and earth-toned bracelets that falsely deceived me into being nervous before I struck up a chat.

In the face of discomfort, I was growing up, triumphing over a mode of business communication that felt entirely foreign. Genuine human interaction is a rarity in the realm of marketing, but I suppose that's the power of music.

It was exhilarating to be working in rooms where I was enveloped by physical artifacts of the artform I loved most. The more I promoted, the more I took note of special editions of historied records and enticing new releases from emerging artists and bands. I'd caress intricately designed casings between my fingers as I browsed, paying respect to the gentle beauty of their tangibility. Being in local record stores brought back buried memories of being in India as a five-year-old when my mom and dad would pick up Bollywood CDs for me from street vendors on chaotic streets that we could play on the car rides home.

Sixteen years later, promoting in record stores was the synthesis of work and play. I would often give in to the cannibalistic impulse of allocating half of my paycheck to records I craved for my own collection. My promo runs were framed by the haunting synth arpeggios of psych-rock quartet Crumb's 2019 record, *Jinx,* which I discovered while promoting in Rough Trade and quickly adopted into my daily routine. When I listen to it now, or stare at the bright, bumblebee yellow LP on my shelf, I hear the sounds of every sunburned adventure I set out on.

By the middle of that summer, the RIAA reported that vinyl sales had generated more than $224 million in revenue.[61] One of the records I helped promote, *Help Us Stranger* by The Raconteurs, had scored a number one on the *Billboard* 200 in July, largely thanks to its success on vinyl, which comprised a staggering 30 percent of overall sales.[62] These trends, although on some level counterintuitive in the digital age, made perfect sense to me. Members of my placeless generation may never feasibly be able to own houses. Why wouldn't we crave the chance to at the very least own some freaking records?

To those of us who have been digitally cultivated, vinyl is appealing because it is an outlet for us to memorialize our musical experiences, immersing ourselves in worlds within defined parameters. Streaming services offer an immediate and overwhelming array of choices, extricated from their original sources. Every physical record, conversely, is a fixed manifestation of nostalgia for a reality we will never access, and an emblem of commitment to a given artist and a body of work.

Gradually, the scariest bullet point on my job description became the centerpiece of my sweaty summer (and the fall and the winter that followed), one that I cherished for its unfamiliar intimacy. I'd wander the blocks of Manhattan South and Williamsburg East like a music plugger from the days of Tin Pan Alley, carrying posters and stickers and pins in an olive-green duffel bag. I was emboldened by my

---

61 Ibid.

62 Caitlyn Kelley, "The Raconteurs' 'Help Us Stranger' Becomes Their First No. 1 Album on the Billboard 200," *Forbes,* June 30, 2019.

assumption of a title that has existed for far longer than the name "Zuckerberg" has held any cultural weight. I'd walk into Rough Trade to hang up posters on the central bulletin board or to cover 250-person shows in its beer-stained backdoor venue, nourished by a sense of complete and utter freedom.

To promote music within microcommunities that I could perceive with my very own eyes was to engage deeply with the results of my actions as opposed to just analyzing impressions from behind a screen.

As my senior year continued, I became increasingly attached to the tradition of my promo runs. Oftentimes, I'd share the experience with friends, seeking their promotional assistance or urging them to bite the bullet and buy that new James Blake record they were eyeing so intensely. Sure, I sometimes still felt like I was in over my head; I didn't quite overcome my nervous tick of pacing up and down the block before walking into Mercer Books & Records to face an employee who never ceased to glare at me with venom. Occasionally, I wondered if a more analytical digital sales internship would have afforded me a sharper attunement to technological trends as opposed to bouncing around from record store to record store. But even in the depths of December, when I could only cling onto my posters with gloved claws under icy breath, I truly loved my job.

Something about my role felt natural, even necessary. We as humans are meant to communicate and collaborate with one another, in business and in life. Since the days of the ancient Athenian bazaar, communication has been a facet of the marketplace. Having this job meant being a part of the evolution of a paradigm that has probably been around for as long as it has because, hey—it really works!

I knew my time working in record stores would be limited to the remainder of my senior year, but it ended up being even more fleeting than I could have ever anticipated. I never knew that the one rushed promo run when I promoted Tennis' record *Swimmer* and their sold-out shows at Brooklyn Steel would be my last before the country went into national lockdown in March 2020. I never knew that I would never have a chance to communicate my gratitude to James and Jamal at Village Music World, or to carry out one last ritualistic stroll around the Brooklyn Inlet Park to admire the skyline before hopping on the L train back to Manhattan.

I never got my closure, but then again, none of us did.

The coronavirus pandemic has ravaged local record store ecosystems globally. In April 2020, *Digital Music News* reported that a wide variety of independent record stores have been forced to shut down, from Dead Media in Minnesota to Bop Street Records in Seattle to Rotten Island Records in Brooklyn, which sits in comatose directly across from me today.[63]

Some retailers will be able to weather this storm. Some have managed to pivot their business models to online websites and door-pickup systems. In a June 2020 *USA Today* report, Doyle Davis, the co-owner of the beloved Nashville record store Grimey's, speaks out about the obstacles the pandemic

---

63 Dylan Smith, "More Indie Record Stores Are Calling It Quits—Steady Sounds, Dead Media Latest," *Digital Music News*, May 25, 2020.

has posed: "[it's] certainly the most challenging situation I've ever faced." That being said, Davis credits online sales and customers' dedication to supporting their communities for keeping his store on life support: "We're still here. We've been able to generate enough revenue to pay rent for now."[64]

"But the point of independent record shops is that they're not websites," says *INDY Week*'s Will Atkinson in a July 2020 article. "They sell an experience, not just a product. The tactile and social nature of record shopping is central in its appeal, which almost certainly contributed to the resurgence of vinyl over the last decade."[65]

Brooklyn based indie-pop duo Dollshot, composed of husband and wife Rosie and Noah Kaplan, are no strangers to the turnover of local music hubs. When I spoke to them, they reminisced about the record stores and venues of New York's yesteryear, lamenting the disintegration of microcommunities that, despite meaning everything to them and their cohorts of artists, have been stomped out by large companies or economic disarray in a seemingly perpetual cycle. As the founders of Underwolf Records, they know firsthand the power of local music economies. Untethered to commercial trends, the pair is dedicated to highlighting artists who, like them, don't necessarily fit the molds that the mainstream music industry perpetuates.

"[The record] is definitely a nonessential item for many people," Rosie tells me. While the duo loves pressing vinyl records, it

---

64 Gary Dinges, "Record Stores Were Already Struggling before the Pandemic. Here's How They're Staying Afloat Now," *USA Today*, June 12, 2020.

65 Will Atkinson, "Record Shops Sell a Hands-on Experience. Now They're Adapting to a Hands-off World.," *INDY Week*, July 8, 2020.

poses an immense economic burden, particularly in the wake of the pandemic, when anything deemed frivolous may not have the space to thrive. "It's scary at this point to do another run not knowing how many could be sold," says Noah, "[but] I'm a huge believer in physical media."

Financial constraints aside, Rosie believes that the pandemic and its isolating effects are making people cherish their physical items increasingly, for "it's really comforting to feel the presence of art."

Daniel Lupton, the owner of the Sorry State record store in Raleigh, North Carolina, is also optimistic about people's heightened reckoning with the value of physical records. "I think people not being able to come into the shop realize what they miss, and they're really interested in making sure that we get through it, that we can get back to normal," he notes in the aforementioned *INDY Week* article.[66]

A phone can carry infinite songs, but sometimes, it's even better to hold just twelve.

Perhaps, one hopeful prospect of the pandemic can be the channeling of our newfound gratitude into structural action, to help ensure that record stores and the local ecosystems they belong to can continue to thrive in the long-term.

The coronavirus vaccine, whenever it arrives, will reintroduce many important aspects of daily life. One that I am selfishly craving is the return of my record stores. I am yearning for

---

66 Ibid.

the music I could touch, the ecosystem I could see with my own eyes. Those record stores were so much more than passageways to buying, selling, and trading. They were artistic archives, family businesses, and most of all, community hubs.

What that special summer and that special job afforded me is a profound appreciation for the value of such local music economies and the ways in which they enriched my understanding and appreciation for music. Their existence has never been more threatened, and yet, I have never been more certain of their purpose and significance across the cultural, social, economic—and personal—spheres.

I'm waiting patiently for the day when I walk by Rotten Island Records and see slivers of sunlight on rows of records, devoid of dust entirely.

PRESERVING MAGIC, PROTECTING LIVELIHOODS

Beyond New Orleans' Musical Escapes

To enter New Orleans is to enter a realm of artistic wizardry. Driven by local subcultures, Louisiana's capital is one of the world's most cherished music cities. Its immersive spirit of creative excellence on every corner is instrumental in what makes it so magical to behold. However, it is this very magic that can mask the hustle and grind of even its most celebrated artists, perceived as a playground for tourists but unacknowledged as a workplace for locals.

Mere months before the coronavirus pandemic transformed the music ecosystem and daily life in the United States, I traveled to Louisiana with my society at NYU Gallatin, the Americas Scholars. My cohort, composed of students whose academic concentrations ranged from environmental policy to criminal justice law to poetry, was tasked with researching the effects of climate change on the region as it related to disaster and remedy. Given my background, I was curious to consider how music communities in New Orleans had fared during natural disasters such as Hurricane Katrina. I wondered about the kinds of bonds that artists formed with one another in a land that had suffered so greatly across generations, defined by its idiosyncratic instability.

Just hours after we landed, three of us decided to brave the January briskness and wander the French Quarter, eager to immerse ourselves into a notoriously sprightly, festive and multicultural city, perhaps America's most eccentric. By dusk, our mouths were coated with powdered sugar, bellies bursting with beignets, flight-fried faces framed by cotton candy sky. We sat on flimsy benches by the fabled Mississippi River, enveloped in the sound of tourist chatter and the melancholic melodies of a kilted bagpipe player. He was elevated on a bronze-hued platform, facing the facade of the tri-towered St. Louis Cathedral as he played, unsolicited but tacitly treasured.

After sunset, we traversed the craggy sidewalk of Chartres Street, gliding by the white-marbled Louisiana Supreme Court Building. We were strolling past antique shops, souvenir kiosks, and balcony bars aplenty when a street corner vocalist stole our attention. Her voice was all-consuming—acrobatic and full-bodied. She belted out a heartbreak ballad, lamenting the loss of love. I could hardly believe that such an incredible musician, as technically impressive as any stadium-filler, was giving us her gift free of cost (barring a barren tip jar by her feet that was as easy to neglect as a stray pebble).

On one hand, stumbling into her was a welcome surprise. Her passion was palpable in every soundwave she produced. On the other hand, something felt uneasy about her position in our lives as background noise, mere atmosphere. Every sound and sight of our evening was eerily dreamlike—it was a fantasy that we silently understood would soon fade.

One day after our run-in with the vocalist, I met up with my friend Morgan Badurak, an aspiring publicist, music industry student at Loyola University New Orleans, and my colleague at Sony Music. Over chicory coffee at a café steps from the river, she expressed to me that the city's musicians are often forced to contend with the widespread public expectation that their art should be freely accessible simply because they are pursuing their passion. Local artists are perceived to have no desire, and by extension, no right, to pursue equitable compensation for their work. Before we left the café after sunset, Morgan and I ruffled through our pockets to locate spare change we could drop off in the hat of a jazz musician who flanked the front door with another impromptu—or perhaps, meticulously-planned—performance. The alluring cliché of artists at play is both a reality and a societal veneer that conceals the veritable struggles of the city's creative community.

Universally recognized as the birthplace of jazz, New Orleans' lineage of musicianship has long served as an avenue for its citizens, a plurality of whom are Black, to transcend the societal barriers of their racial statuses.[67] Music pervades nearly every aspect of the city's culture; the jazz funeral is a staple of any grieving process, and an audience's seamless inclusion in the tradition of a Mardi Gras second line is taken, gleefully, for granted.[68] As my peers and I experienced firsthand, musi-

---

67   "New Orleans, Louisiana Population 2020," US Cities, World Population Review, accessed October 14, 2020.

68   Bruce Boyd Raeburn, "'They're Tryin' to Wash Us Away': New Orleans Musicians Surviving Katrina," *Journal of American History*, 94 (Dec.

cians adorn the streets each evening, offering celebration to any and all passersby, neighbors, and visitors alike.

This singular musical heritage has been remarkably resilient. The city's localized traditions have persisted against financially motivated pressures from the global music industry to scale up, centuries of political mismanagement and governmental corruption, and perhaps most crucially, the ever-looming danger of environmental doom. According to a May 2020 article in *The Washington Post*, coastal Louisiana has lost nearly a quarter of its landmass in the last century as a result of rising sea levels, exacerbated by the agendas of oil giants who are irreverent of the communities that climate destruction impacts most.[69]

Beyond gradual environmental decay, the natural catastrophe that was 2005's Hurricane Katrina, and the city's subsequent levee failures, robbed many musical artists of their jobs, their instruments, and in some cases, even their homes. "Katrina exposed the fallacy of the city's 'good time' ethos," notes Bruce Boyd Raeburn, the curator of the Hogan Jazz Archive at Tulane University, in his December 2007 paper in the *Journal of American History*. The hurricane spawned "serious implications for its musical culture, rooted in the festival traditions of Black neighborhoods that were largely destroyed."[70] The principal arbiters of the city's culture were displaced in life and in art.

2007): 812–819.

69 Chris Mooney, "Loss of Louisiana Marshes That Protect New Orleans Is 'Probably Inevitable,' Study Finds," *The Washington Post*, May 22, 2020.

70 Raeburn, *Journal of American History*.

Fifteen years post-Katrina, the core of New Orleans' creative spirit remains, and the city regularly enjoys artistic renaissances. However, musicians still face financial challenges despite their central role in fortifying the city's economy. According to a 2012 survey by Sweet Home New Orleans, a musicians advocacy group, the average musician in New Orleans makes just $17,800 a year.[71] Furthermore, the financial and cultural devastation of the live economy halting phenomenon that is the coronavirus pandemic has been simply incalculable for a city that normally averages eighty-five musical events per day.[72]

In a 2017 article written by Sarah Aggour, music veteran and project manager at the Recording Academy Reid Wick comments on the societal underappreciation of music's commercial role in New Orleans: "the banking leaders, the business leaders, the elected leaders … I don't think that they really value what the music community brings from an economic standpoint … a lot of it has been taken for granted because we've always been here."[73]

Whenever artists are lucky enough to achieve notable levels of success, they often have no choice but to move away and set up lives in major music markets, typically on either coast, forced to leave behind the communities that shaped them: "It hurts me to see artists have to leave here to go to a Nashville, to go to an Atlanta or Los Angeles,"

---

71 Jan Ramsey, "By the Numbers: Sweet Home New Orleans Releases 2012 State of the New Orleans Music Community Report," *OffBeat Magazine*, May 1, 2013.

72 David Montgomery, "In a Self-Isolated World, New Orleans Musicians Fight to Beat Back the Silence," *The Washington Post*, April 9, 2020.

73 Sarah Aggour, "New Orleans: The Culture of Resilient Music Arises After Katrina," *PCD Network*, April 10, 2017.

says DJ Raj Smoove, a local producer and artist, when interviewed by *NOLA.com* columnist Chelsea Brasted in January 2019. "Our artists should be able to provide for themselves by their craft in their city beyond the live music we're known for."[74]

During our trip, my society had an opportunity to interact with members of the Preservation Hall Jazz Band, a world-distinguished ensemble founded by tubist and entrepreneur Allan Jaffe in the early 1960s, for a short performance and intimate discussion.[75] "These days artists don't get teachers—they get publicists," mused the group's bandleader as he differentiated the musical landscape in New Orleans from the rest of the country to our cohort. As he spoke, I couldn't help but grin and think of so many of my young peers in the music business, most notably my publicist friend. She hopes, in her profession, to protect these kinds of artists through the mechanism of a more robust and wide-reaching local music industry. Yet notions of "industry" hardly exist in these musicians' vocabularies. They are far too concerned with their craft to place importance in commerce. As is the case in music hubs around the world, the artists and the advocates who aim to support them suffer from speaking different languages.

While the band serenaded us, we sat in two lines, crisscrossed in a wooden and damp rehearsal room on St. Peter Street in the center of the French Quarter. The sweet sound of virtuosic

---

74 Chelsea Brasted, "There Are Gaps in New Orleans' Music Industry. Business Leaders Hope to Fill Them," *NOLA.com*, January 25, 2019.

75 "Our Story," About, Preservation Hall, accessed October 14, 2020.

saxophone was a refuge from days of emotionally cumbersome research lectures and wetland expeditions that educated us on the imminent natural disasters and strains of political disillusionment that plague the region.

Like the vocalist we had encountered days before, Preservation Hall was offering us an electrifying escape. They were soulful and spontaneous, communicating with one another using the kinds of seamless visual and sonic cues that can only emerge from lifelong discipline and determination. From the hits of Bunk Johnson and Kate Smith to the instantly recognizable New Orleans staple "When the Saints Go Marching In," they delighted us with the music they championed most. For one hour, we entered a world devoid of peril, drunk on the harmonies of masters honing their craft.

Our nights on the historic Frenchmen Street, bursting with cacophonous crowds and venues, were similarly euphoric. We danced under neon red glow, shouting out requests and swinging our hips to sax solos on jam-packed, cocktail-stained dance floors. The artists downed shots between sets, urging us to do the same; we (of-age) scholars happily obliged. In those moments of bliss, it often felt like New Orleans' artistic community was in some way immune to the broader injustices that affected the city and state, always available to whisk away its subjects, often tourists like ourselves, onto sonic and experiential adventures. It was easy to forget the creative individuals and teams who shed sweat to conjure up the magic of our experience, to, again and again, neglect the instability they regularly battled.

Some organizations, such as the New Orleans Music Economy Initiative organized by the Greater New Orleans Regional

Economic Development team, aim to reshape the culture of musical consumption in the city through comprehensive economic analysis and development efforts. The project cites the expertise of Sound Diplomacy, a global music policy consultancy, to develop strategies that will optimize the local industry's economic capacities by filling in its commercial gaps. Such an endeavor would entail the generation (and protection) of robust jobs across the music ecosystem, ranging from intellectual property management to publishing to label services to every other type of business resource that is routinely offered within the major music markets.[76]

"No artist can do it alone. They need lawyers, publishers, managers, marketing—it's a whole ecosystem and economy that develops just from music," notes DJ Raj Smoove in the aforementioned *NOLA.com* article. "We've always been known for our music in New Orleans. It's about time we're known for our music industry."[77] Without such structural intervention, New Orleans' artistic communities might see losses not schematically unlike the land loss that threatens the Louisiana wetlands.

In many ways, such movements feel essential, even uplifting. But as an outsider, who am I to claim that something as historied as New Orleans' music scene needs any fortification from suits and spectators like you and me? Will such developments ultimately support the artistic integrity of street corner vocalists and community-oriented bands, or will it

---

76 "New Orleans Music Economy Initiative (NOME)," New Orleans, Sound Diplomacy, accessed October 14, 2020.

77 Brasted, *NOLA.com*.

force such artists to conform to global, algorithmic standards? The ultimate challenge for the wielders of power will be to figure out how to simultaneously instate economic stability for New Orleans' artists while still preserving the local spirit that has given the city's music its incomparable character.

In the meantime, nonprofit organizations such as the New Orleans Musicians' Clinic will continue to cultivate a safety net for the city's artists by providing medical care for artists, regardless of insurance status or ability to pay, as they have since 1998.[78] As the crises continue, their socially-oriented services will remain indispensable.

To bastardize New Orleans' musical spirit would be to stifle the unbounded creativity that has earned it its iconic reputation around the world. But to simply accept and extoll it as an escape may not—and perhaps never has been—enough.

---

78 "About Us," New Orleans Musicians' Clinic, accessed October 14, 2020.

FALSE INHERITANCE

The Oversaturation of the Self-Titled Album

This is who I really am. Do you believe me?

Ah, the quixotic query that an artist proposes when they decide to name an album after themselves. Usually, we listeners have never expressed an interest in providing an answer to this question—why should we do the work of defining *your* work?—yet still, the trend persists, New Music Friday after Friday after Friday.

The self-titled album is as old as the commercial music industry. Since the smog-ridden dusks of Tin Pan Alley (the late nineteenth-century and early twentieth-century community of NYC music publishers and songwriters who dominated popular music in the United States), artists and bands have attached their monikers to their projects in a righteous effort to spoon-feed their identities to their listeners.[79]

As an introductory effort, this strategy often proves productive. From *The Doors* (1967) to *Led Zeppelin* (1969) to *Madonna*

---

79 The Editors of Encyclopaedia Britannica, "Tin Pan Alley," *Encyclopædia Britannica*, February 27, 2020.

(1983) to *Taylor Swift* (2006) to *Vampire Weekend* (2008) to *Every-Aspiring-Acoustic-Singer-Songwriter-Ever* (∞), the linking of the debut album to the driver of the machine can be a worthy marriage of form and content.[80]

Vampire Weekend's proclivity for Ivy-League allusions, Taylor Swift's autobiographical voice, and Madonna's synthetic power choruses are all stylistic notions that have underlined the trajectories of these artists' careers ever since their initial inclusions, revitalized constantly as reference points for the public's dissection. In such cases, an artist passing down their name to their firstborn makes more than enough sense.

However, it is self-titled albums that appear once the race has long begun that perplex me. What is it about your *fifth* son that warrants the inheritance of your name? A mid-career self-title is designed to be daring, to roar of reformulation, redirection, reinvention. It's obnoxiously decisive, a *look-at-me* that no real fan could dare ignore. It is to say, *you've had it all wrong, this is what it's all about. All that crap that came before this was just to prepare for this moment.* Once you've done it, it is done. Done! Done! *Donnez-moi votre attention*, it bleeds.

But which self does a middle-aged self-title refer to? Paramore's *Paramore* popped up at a point in the band's history when it seemed the least like it*self,* having recently lost two of its founding members, with lead-singer Hayley Williams openly suffering from a bout of depression and deep

---

80 Yasmine Lomax, "What's the Deal with Self-Titled Albums?" *Yasmine Lorax* (blog), August 11, 2019.

disillusionment with the industry.[81] Demi Lovato's *Demi* was characterized by its confessional ballads chronicling the former *Barney*-star's triumphant journey to sobriety, although she later revealed she had been relapsing throughout the album cycle.[82] Perhaps, the designation of a self-title is merely a marker of resignation, an ideal standing in for a fully realized self while positioning itself as the latter. *I don't know who I am, or what this is, who maybe you can help me figure it out,* it weeps.

When we're sold the promise that a work is meant to be the pinnacle of an artist's self-consciousness and creative fruition, any hints of inconsistency engender suspicion, or at the very least, collective eye-rolls.

Even in the case when a middle-child-self-incarnation is widely praised (Arctic Monkeys and the remaining Beatles certainly aren't losing sleep over past nomenclature), I can't help but wonder what potential has been stifled by the choice not to give such albums independent classifications. If *Beyoncé* is Queen B's seminal work, as is indicated by the implications of its title, what do we make of *Lemonade*? If *Charli* is Charli XCX's mission statement, what do superfans have left to look forward to when the clubs are back in season?

Aren't artists, and the teams that support them, getting ahead of themselves, naming albums after what they ideally might

---

81 Matthew Scott Donnelly, "Paramore Bassist Quits, One Original Member Remains," *Pop Crush,* December 15, 2015.

82 Casey Fitzsimmons, "The Most Jaw-Dropping Moments from Demi Lovato's Documentary," *Soundigest,* October 24, 2017.

represent out in the soundscape, as opposed to what they veritably are in their heads?

Perhaps, during the days when music discovery was relegated to record stores, self-titled albums were a seamless marketing tool, a signpost of selfhood. But in the age of Spotify Canvas backgrounds, Instagram livestreams, and Reddit Ask-Me-Anythings, artists don't need to distill their projects to their bylines to impose their identities. Perhaps my umbrage is better suited for the decision makers in Capitol Tower (hire me, please!) than the platform-heeled pop stars at Shangri-La Studios, who just want to communicate their art at the level that they created it.

Regardless, I hope I fail to see the day when Lady Gaga unleashes a "Stefani," or Tame Impala a "Kevin." If you take the superhero cape off, do it gently, in your walk-in, and not on the sidewalk; don't dampen the imagination you once ignited in our heads. Use yours instead.

BOLLYWOOD, CALIFORNIA

Navigating Cultural Appropriation as an ABCD

"Cultures overlap and intersect in various complex ways. A single person may belong to a variety of cultures simultaneously."
—JAMES O. YOUNG IN *CULTURAL APPROPRIATION AND THE ARTS*[83]

It is with much reluctance and a painful sigh that I sit here today and declare to you that I am, in many ways, the quintessential "ABCD": an American Born Confused Desi.

Not thrown around particularly fondly, the term, popularized by the 2001 film *American Desi* that you've likely never heard of, is meant to identify those of us Indian Americans who were raised in the United States by immigrant parents.[84]

---

83 James O. Young, *Cultural Appropriation and the Arts* (Malden: Blackwell Publishing, 2009), 13.

84 Kishwer Vikaas, "ABCD: Who Are You Calling Confused?" *Asian American Writers' Workshop,* July 24, 2014.

We're not entirely Indian—we grew up enveloped in the realm of after-school McDonald's, reality TV stars on grocery store tabloids, and twinges of red-white-and-blue patriotism a couple times a year—yet we're not entirely American either, having matured in households that cherished lentil-oriented dishes, Sanskrit-based dialects, textiled outfits, and dedication to age-old family traditions.

Collectively, we struggle to balance these divergent identities.

One way to look at it is that we are "culturally inadequate and unfinished," with no real sense of belonging.[85] A more encouraging perspective is that we've had the privilege of being immersed in two different spheres of this massive planet, equipped for the diverse and nuanced environments we now face as self-sufficient and secure global citizens. I wish I could tell you that the latter proposition has always been my reality, but as I creep up the ladder of my twenties, it continues to feel like an ultimate goal rather than something I've already achieved.

For the past several years, my identity crisis seems to be reflected in the music I consume and the societies I inhabit. Creative entities that I once understood as entirely disparate have begun to converge on the biggest stages as globalization heightens—you can imagine my confusion as I watched American-born former Disney-Channel-Champ Selena Gomez lip-sync her way through a pop song accompanied by *tabla* with a *sari* draped around her body and a *bindi* on

---

85 Vijay Prashad, *The Karma of Brown Folk* (Minneapolis: U of Minnesota, 2000), 131.

her forehead on an American MTV stage as a ninth-grader in April 2013 (Phew!).

My ABCD heart could barely handle the spectacle, and as Indian music is likely to be the next gargantuan global influence to impact American music, there's far more confusion in order—it's probably best that I start from the beginning.

PHASE ONE: PRIDE

By the time I had grown into a sentient being, I had already been dipped into the culture of Bollywood, the colossal Indian film industry that produces about a thousand movie-musicals a year, give or take a few hundred. Bollywood is zestful, uproarious, and enlivened by song and dance. In fact, a Bollywood flick is only as good as its soundtrack; film music drives approximately 80 percent of overall music revenue in India, dominating the airwaves and charts.[86]

Since soundtracks often dictate whether an audience will be inclined to see a given film, India's music and film industries are fundamentally intertwined. These larger-than-life musicals both illustrate and influence modern Indian society, shaping the sociocultural ethos of the world's second-biggest population. Bollywood fans are devoted; they learn every lyric of the songs, imitate the sharable choreography, and admire the intricate outfits they see reflected in the widespread media they consume. Albeit subcultural in a global

---

86 Cherie Hu, "How India, the Global Music Industry's Sleeping Giant, Is Finally Waking Up," *Forbes*, September 23, 2017.

context, Bollywood appeals to India's "mainstream"; its biggest stars pervade quotidian life, projected onto theater screens, plastered on billboards, flattened on the side of Coke bottles, and heralded on printouts in prayer rooms. These films establish trends, break barriers, wield political importance, and captivate millions.

Very rarely in Hollywood does a movie come along that is so societally impactful that almost every citizen, regardless of class, age, race, or personal identity, is acutely aware of it as an ineluctable cultural experience. Bollywood produces about a dozen or so of those each year, with songs that are so widely diffused that they'd send "Shallow" from Bradley Cooper and Lady Gaga's *A Star Is Born* into shipwreck.

The music of Bollywood is meant for the masses, yet it is based on the foundation of a lesser-known, traditional discipline. Indian classical music is one of the world's oldest musical phenomena, and it relies on an encyclopedic notation system and a rubric of originative melodic techniques that have had an undeniable influence on Eastern and Western artistic trailblazers alike, from Chennai's A.R. Rahman to Liverpool's George Harrison.

The hyper-commercialized Bollywood apparatus has reaped the benefits of adopting the droning, earthy instrumentation and rich improvisational vocal techniques that are routinely employed in Indian classical music. Bollywood anthems often maintain the core auditory components of the traditional artform, such as the use of microtones and ornamental *alankar*, while applying them to rhythmically accelerated structures that appeal to the general public.

By the age of six, my parents had put me in Indian vocal classical lessons, an initiative to keep me connected to their homeland. As such, until I was about ten years old, listening to Bollywood and other Indian music exclusively was the norm for me. The first song my infant ears ever processed was one in Hindi, not English. While my classmates were rocking out to Green Day, I was likely learning songs and dances from 1998's *Devdas*, a blockbuster Bollywood tragedy that my older sister and I adored.

This didn't mean that I was disenfranchised from American culture—I was obsessed with American sports cars, had a fairly, archetypal California accent, dude, like, you know? I wore Levi's and the occasional Abercrombie shirt, like my friends. I carried myself in the same way that the people around me did.

However, it was clear where my true affinity rested.

When white people seemed to embrace Indian culture, I felt validated. I craved any opportunity to show my peers Bollywood movies and songs, begging my friends with short attention spans to endure hours of subtitled musical galore. I was thrilled to perform Indian classical music for my teachers and fellow students at talent shows in school, and even if someone told me they were a fan of *samosas* and *chicken tikka masala*, I felt obligated to thank them and blush. To me, it was a personal compliment (yikes).

If a famous Bollywood actor were to be interviewed by Jay Leno or briefly featured in a thirty-second cameo on an ABC drama, I cheered them on like a proud soccer mom. I convinced my friends to come to my family's annual Diwali parties decked out in *kurtas* and *saris*—bonus points if they donned *bindis* and *kumkum* powder. Back then, I was overjoyed to share an inherent facet of myself with people who I assumed would never be exposed to it without my guidance.

Since Bollywood culture was negligible in American pop culture, undiscovered by most, I embraced my role as a liaison. I was proud to enable something beyond White America, the "mainstream" of the river I inhabited. Perhaps, I was eager to facilitate this cultural exchange because nothing was being taken away from me. I had invited the outsiders in; I was in control.

PHASE TWO: VULNERABILITY

With age, the glorious relationship that I had once had with my Indian roots faltered in the predictable sort of way that my elementary-school self would have scoffed at.

The musical whitewashing began when I moved on from my SanDisk to my first iPod, introduced to the glorious playground that was US iTunes. With an 8 GB storage limit to contain me, out went Bollywood, and in came the Western flood. I didn't grow up on the Beatles and the Stones and Stevie Wonder and early Coldplay, so as a young teenager, I made up for lost time by submerging myself in the musical legacies of those artists. I became less invested in keeping up to date with the release of every new Bollywood soundtrack and more inclined to take steps to fit into the environments I inhabited every day.

This gradual period of development during which I gained so much knowledge and respect for America and lost so much of my ardor for India is hazy in retrospect. I barely knew myself then, and looking back, it's still difficult for me to resituate myself in the mindset of such a nebulous phase of life. All I know is that at one point or another around my fourteenth year of existence, I discovered that I hardly knew how to speak or understand Hindi anymore, a realization that dispirited my Bollywood obsessed aunt when I visited one weekend without a single recommendation for movie night.

With the introduction of Western music into my artistic repertoire, my weekly Indian vocal lessons began to feel more like a chore than a privilege. At home, I opted for pasta instead of traditional home-cooked *roti* and *daal*. When strangers asked me where I was from, I no longer prefaced my responses with "Well, my parents are from India, but …". Subconsciously, my loyalties had shifted. I had learned to prefer when white people just saw me as one of them: an American. No cultural exchange necessary. My Indianness was a flower patch I let wilt, not out of explicit resentment, but simply out of neglect.

Around this time, I opened up my eyes and saw that the pop music industry decided to rescue the flowers that I had abandoned and shove them into American soil. In April 2013, former Disney Channel star Selena Gomez released her first solo single, "Come & Get It," a fairly predictable pop record with a few key singularities. The song opens and closes with a sample of a male Indian classical voice singing Punjabi over the fast-paced beat of a *tabla*, the principal Indian percussive instrument.[87] During the

---

[87] "Selena Gomez - Come & Get It," WhoSampled, accessed October 14, 2020.

promotional cycle of the song, Gomez was photographed wearing Indian attire and jewelry and incorporating Indian dance techniques into her performance pieces. Most contentiously, she donned a *bindi*, an ancient Hindu symbol, throughout the campaign.[88]

This was far from the first time that mainstream America had decided to draw influence from the evergreen melting pot of Indian culture—from a teenaged Gwen Stefani to a late-90s Madonna, notable American pop-cultural figures have been sporting Indian accessories for decades—but Gomez's take on the trend was one of the first times I had witnessed this intermixture as a conscious human being, a soon-to-be young adult.

When I heard the song, I was optimistic about the prospect of a fusion between the two worlds that I had found so difficult to straddle. Maybe, American adoption of Bollywood techniques could be an answer to the internal dilemmas I was facing. While I enjoyed the song's earworm exterior on a superficial level, I got the sense in my lower stomach that some sort of injustice had been enacted. Hearing classical Indian instruments laid over a cliché pop beat on the radio felt sinister, a break away from the validation of yesteryear. Instead, it was a jarring reminder that a thing that had once served as my own chance at uniqueness was no longer all that unique, a costume at the disposal of the more powerful—and maybe no longer mine at all.

---

88 Donna Kaufman, "Should Selena Gomez Apologize for Wearing a Bindi at the MTV Movie Awards?" *Today*, April 17, 2013.

In an interview with Ryan Seacrest, Gomez discussed the track's "tribal, Middle eastern feel."[89] Weeks later, she pinpointed the record "as European ... [with] a lot of island-y sounds."[90] Yet to my trained ears and to the ears of so many others, the sound was unmistakably Indian. What gave her the right to stake a claim in a sound she couldn't even define beyond its exotic quality? On the other hand, what grounds did I have to make a case against her? This time, I didn't have much agency at all.

Reactions from the rest of the South Asian community were mixed. An Indian-born former classmate of mine at NYU who wishes to remain anonymous believes that Gomez and her team portrayed Indian musical and aesthetic techniques "very poorly. They used Bollywood influences just to make the song seem more outlandish and just to attract more people to view the video than to actually represent the culture."

It was hard for me, too, to decipher why a white-passing Hispanic-American like Gomez would want to don traditional Indian garb and employ Indian instrumentation (while crooning lyrics about seduction concocted by a strategic team of songwriters), other than to use our culture as an accessory to command attention. Another former classmate of mine, Krishna Gaur, who immigrated to the US for college after living in India for her entire childhood, sees the record in a

---

89 Ryan Seacrest, "Selena Gomez Premieres 'Come & Get It' PART 1 | Interview | On Air with Ryan Seacrest," On Air with Ryan Seacrest, uploaded on April 8, 2013, YouTube video, 4:55.

90 Zaydra Rivera, "Selena Gomez Urged to Apologize for Wearing Hindu Religious Ornament during MTV Performance," *NY Daily News*, April 16, 2013.

more positive light: "It actually feels nice that our music is getting recognition because it's so under-appreciated." However, even she has her reservations: "I like the way [Gomez] incorporated the music. But the *bindi* shit—that was weird."

Some critics, such as the members of the Universal Society of Hinduism, are less equivocal in their stance: "The bindi on the forehead is an ancient tradition in Hinduism and has religious significance," says Hindu statesman Rajan Zed, as reported by the Huffington Post in April 2013. "It is an auspicious religious and spiritual symbol. ... It is not meant to be thrown around loosely."[91]

A year later, then-emerging rapper Iggy Azalea released her music video for "Bounce," a more odious example of a critical failure to appreciate, rather than appropriate. Although neither the song's lyrics nor its sonic composition make any allusions whatsoever to Indian culture, the song's accompanying video features Azalea clad in colorful wedding garb, surrounded by a horde of young Indian backup dancers who mirror her every choreographed move.[92] Naturally, the video's release was met with a well-earned slew of critical indignation. Writer Rohin Guha, in an April 2013 essay for *The Aerogram*, begs his readers to consider "Bounce's complicated question: Are we okay with the fact that Western pop culture has transformed the culture of Indian people—a subset of people who make up one-fifth of the world's population—into a wearable commodity, worthy of imitation only when fashion dictates and

---

91 Cavan Sieczkowski, "Selena Gomez Bindi: Hindu Leaders Demand Apology for MTV Movie Awards Costume," *HuffPost*, April 16, 2013.

92 Iggy Azalea, "Iggy Azalea - Bounce (Official Music Video)," Iggy Azalea, uploaded on May 5, 2013, YouTube video, 3:16.

otherwise disposable? More importantly, what does it mean that white people can wear Indian culture like drag and be hailed as trendy while South Asian people—born into this culture—continue being Othered?"[93]

Surely, Azalea and her team should have foreseen that plastering a white face as the focal point in a sea of brown would be no welcome sight for South Asian viewers. Halfway through the video, a fleeting picture of the Taj Mahal flashes across the screen in between clips of Azalea dancing, a flippant and futile addition to an already chaotic conglomeration of lazy stereotypes.[94] The injustice I perceived while watching the video triggered in me a defensiveness that was almost as reassuring as it was fervent; I knew that my inclination to protect this culture had to stem from some sort of deep-rooted affinity that was not all gone. Perhaps the flowers were beginning to bloom again.

On the other side of the spectrum are videos like Coldplay's "Hymn for the Weekend," released in January 2016 during my high school senior spring. While controversial, it has been an outlet for gratification as opposed to contempt for many Indians, including myself. The video purports to portray India in action, showcasing busy streets, children playing in rural habitats, and jubilant local celebrations, primarily centered on the country's annual festival of color, Holi. An homage, rather than a caricature, the video, featuring Beyoncé posing as a vintage Bollywood star, draws parallels to Bollywood

---

93 Rohin Guha, "Iggy Azalea Bounces Backwards with Disappointing Clichés," *The Aerogram*, May 28, 2013.

94 Azalea, "Bounce," YouTube video.

movies that I have fawned over in the past, as well as more traditional facets of Indian culture.[95]

Admittedly, it is neither an artistic masterpiece nor an international relations breakthrough. In their portrayal of village life, Coldplay glosses over many of India's contemporary realities, perpetuating some all too familiar tropes. Regardless, watching the video ignited in me a sense of Indian pride; this Western medium offered understanding, instead of disrespect or mere validation.

MTV News reporter Deepa Lakshmin calls Coldplay's efforts "a great leap forward" due to the fact that "clear efforts were made to respect and celebrate India's culture. The video features residents from Mumbai's Worli Village, and even though Coldplay and Bey are doing their thing, it's the kids that bring life and excitement to the song … in HFTW, the musicians feel secondary to the community in which they're performing."[96] The band was deliberate in their decision to use India as a backdrop for their artistic endeavor, and furthermore, determined to do so in a well-informed and reverent way. Not every viewer would agree with me, but I, for one, am grateful for the video's attempt at authenticity.

---

95 Coldplay, "Coldplay - Hymn for the Weekend (Official Video)," Coldplay, uploaded on January 29, 2016, YouTube video, 4:20.

96 Deepa Lakshmin. "I Was in India When Coldplay and Beyoncé's Video Dropped -- and I Don't See Cultural Appropriation," *MTV News*, February 4, 2016.

PHASE THREE: CERTAIN UNCERTAINTY

In recent years, the Latin music and K-pop frameworks have dominated astounding amounts of real estate on the American and global charts. I posit that Indian music is next in line. Given India's rich artistic and cultural lineage and the sheer number of Indians who have integrated abroad (hi, parents!), such a cultural shift seems inevitable. On the precipice of a potential Indian music revolution, it is worth considering what differentiates cultural appropriation from cultural appreciation. When, if ever, is cultural appropriation acceptable—from artists, businesses, and citizens alike?

The most diplomatic answer I could hope to provide is that there is none. Cultures are emotionally driven, subjective, nuanced, and very difficult, if not impossible, to responsibly define. No one person could ever categorically delineate when it is or when it is not okay for someone to embrace a given form of art; there are simply too many pertinent variables to consider.

Dr. James O. Young, a philosophy scholar and the author of *Cultural Appropriation and the Arts*, holds a "sincere belief [that certain types] of appropriation can be responsible for opening up avenues of communication between cultures. ... Artists who appropriate from other cultures, and the audiences of these artists, often come to have a greater appreciation of the value of other ways of living."[97] A given person might feel disrespected by an outside force infringing upon their culture. Is there a logical way to invalidate said person's feelings? Similarly, could

---

97   James O. Young, *Cultural Appropriation and the Arts*. (Malden: Blackwell Publishing, 2009), 13.

that person logically articulate exactly why outside usage of their artform is impermissible? (I know I couldn't). Is logic even relevant at all? One man's theft is another man's enlightenment. One woman's flattery is another woman's abuse. One man's pride is another woman's vulnerability.

The variables we can assess are the intentions, degrees of respect, and historical implications being considered on either side of the equation. Furthermore, we must ensure to champion the perspectives of the very cultural agents who are attached to the art's origins instead of seeking out ways to dismiss them. Even with these criteria, the answer remains woefully uncertain—but still essential to examine.

Similarly, there is no straightforward answer as to whether or not I lack a clear identity, or if I am a composite of both countries that I am "from." Maybe I'll forever be caught somewhere in the middle, constantly having to assess who I am and what experiences have shaped me. Maybe I am in fact culturally inadequate and unfinished, yet better equipped for the world just the same. Maybe those first four scarlet letters of the alphabet don't have to subsume my sense of self; maybe, I can simply take them in my stride. This limbo is not the easiest place to be in—but it certainly keeps me listening for what's next.

WHY BLAME BILLIE EILISH?

Confronting the Convention of Industry Planting

Dually disruptive and traditional, Billie Eilish is epitomized by her contradictory nature. Her inability to be reduced to a single identity is precisely what makes her so polarizing, and perhaps, so captivating, to millions—myself included.

When we imagine an artist who has "made it," we often conjure up images of unwavering cultural domination. We envision golden GRAMMYs, number ones on the *Billboard* Hot 100, *Saturday Night Live* opening slots, vibrant *Vogue* covers, *BBC* Live Lounge performances, and *Forbes* end-of-year fanfare. In 2020, however, making it in music can often mean something much more subcultural. The chance of a single artist capturing each and every aspect of the zeitgeist—from TV screens to print spreads to social media scrolls—is infinitesimal during an era when people's attention is fragmented into individualized playlists and curated corners of content.

However, within modern music's herd of horses, Billie Eilish is the unicorn to achieve true ubiquity.

To step foot into a music business class during my first year of college in 2016 was to overhear murmurs about Eilish. Nearly every industry analyst who hypothesized about music's potential futures mentioned her name during class presentations. Long before she summoned the scrutiny of the public, Eilish had industry hotshots salivating across the music ecosystem.

Four years later, she has become a bona fide Generation Z superstar. Some believe she is the first mainstream musical prodigy born in the twenty-first century, precocious as both an artist and a public persona.

At the sixty-second Grammy Awards in 2020, she swept five awards, including all four of the major categories, mere months after her eighteenth birthday.[98] In April 2019, she broke the record for the most simultaneously charted *Billboard* Hot 100 titles for a woman in the history of the chart, following the seismic launch of her long-teased debut album, WHEN WE ALL FALL ASLEEP, WHERE DO WE GO?[99]

Dave Grohl, the front man of Foo Fighters, extolled Eilish as a beacon of hope for the artist community, comparing her ascension to that of Nirvana in the early nineties. "'Is rock dead?' When I look at someone like Billie Eilish, rock and roll is not *close* to dead!" he proclaimed proudly to an audience of music executives at a business conference in

---

98 Paul Grein, "Grammys 2020: Billie Eilish Becomes the First Woman to Sweep the Big Four Grammys in One Night," *Billboard,* January 27, 2020.

99 Xander Zellner, "Billie Eilish Earns First Hot 100 Top 10, Breaks Record for Most Simultaneous Hits Among Women," *Billboard,* April 9, 2019.

Los Angeles.[100] Similarly, hip-hop super-producer Timbaland publicly voiced his prediction that Eilish would serve as the dominating musical force of the turn of the decade.[101] Those who champion Eilish praise her for redefining what it means to be an artist in the digital age, inventively representing online youth culture and taking sonic risks that reimagine the aesthetic traditions of commercially-oriented music.

Naturally, Eilish's achievements have been accompanied by brewing contention amongst dedicated music listeners, influential critics, and casual fans alike. A fierce flock of detractors accuses her of commodifying teenage depression in a nefariously performative way to elevate the shock value of her understated music. Others find her genre-bending tendencies insincere, a haphazard appropriation of underrepresented subcultures.

Above all else, Eilish's disparagers rush to label her as an "industry plant," a socially weaponized term that *Complex* defines as "a pithy derogative that [critics] wield to imply that a rapper or singer is an upstart fraud, a record label puppet, a focus group-tested vessel of creativity so-called … any musician with a hazy or straight-up fabricated origin story."[102]

---

100 Michael Roffman, "Dave Grohl on Billie Eilish: 'The Same Thing Is Happening with Her That Happened with Nirvana in 1991'," *Consequence of Sound*, February 13, 2019.

101 The Music Network Staff, "Becoming Billie: How Apple Music and Spotify Helped Make Billie Eilish Music's New Gen Z Superstar," *The Music Network*, April 2, 2019.

102 Justin Charity, "What Is an Industry Plant?" *Complex*, October 20, 2016.

As the scope of Eilish's influence has expanded, I have observed a common dilemma in the discourse that surrounds her: is she a visionary pioneer or a predictably manufactured archetype of a pop star? How much of her success can be attributed to artistic and social authenticity, and how much of it comes from the corporate music industry predetermining her status as a music megastar?

While those on either side of the debate often make claims in a binary fashion, I contend that the notion that she is an organic artist is not at odds with the notion that she has benefited greatly from institutional support. The Western music landscape has a longstanding history of elitist gatekeeping as a determinant of artistic trends, from far back in 375 BC when Plato asserted his ideal role of music in society in *Republic* to the twentieth century's massive wave of music commercialization.[103] To blame an individual player in a well-established game is to ignore the systemic traditions that she is encased in—especially when her prefrontal cortex is years away from being fully developed.

*　*　*

Like me, Eilish is a Los Angeles native. The child of actor parents who took on regional theater and voice-acting projects to support their family, she grew up in a two-bedroom bungalow in the working-class neighborhood of Highland Park. She was homeschooled alongside her older brother,

---

103　Edith Hamilton and Huntington Cairns, *The Collected Dialogues of Plato* (Princeton: Princeton University Press, 1989); David Suisman, *Selling Sounds: The Commercial Revolution in American Music* (Cambridge: Harvard University Press, 2009).

Finneas O'Connell, who went on to garner minor roles on TV staples including *Glee* and *Modern Family* before pursuing a solo music career.[104]

Despite being associated with the entertainment industry, neither Eilish's parents nor her brother ever became household names, certainly never nabbing notable wealth or fame. However, Eilish did have the uncommon privilege of being encouraged to concentrate on her musical interests from a young age. According to her father, Patrick O'Connell, an important pillar of their tight-knit family dynamic was that "they'd been allowed to pursue the things that they were interested in."[105]

Eilish's mother taught her children how to write songs. Eilish's father introduced them to the discographies of established icons, ranging from the Beatles to Linkin Park.[106] Instead of math tests and history papers, the pair were raised on chorus recitals and dance classes, motivated by their parents to hone their creative spirits above all else.

While some see Eilish's well-trained background as reason enough to validate her artistry, others flag it as an indication of the abundance of resources that she has had access to, providing her with an unfair pedestal upon which to stand.

Eilish's brother was her very first and ultimately most crucial collaborator. Her debut single, "Ocean Eyes," was written

---

104 Katie Bain, "A Day in the Life of Billie Eilish," *LNWY*, October 5, 2017.

105 Joe Coscarelli, "Billie Eilish Is Not Your Typical 17-Year-Old Pop Star. Get Used to Her," *The New York Times*, March 28, 2019.

106 Bain, "A Day in the Life," *LNWY*.

entirely by him. He believed her ethereal, emotionally penetrative soprano was better suited for the melancholy track than his voice.[107] The track became the catalyst for attention from music industry executives after a Soundcloud launch in October 2015 that flooded record label and music supervisor inboxes. By August 2016, Eilish had parlayed an artist development deal with discovery platform Platoon into a record deal with Darkroom Records, a label and artist management company controlled by Universal Music Group's Interscope Records, home to heavyweights like Lady Gaga and Gwen Stefani.[108]

To this day, O'Connell remains the lead producer and sole co-writer on all of Eilish's music, which they generate together in a makeshift studio in their cluttered childhood home: "Me and him were both doing the same thing in the same house and just were, like, we live three feet away from each other—why don't we do this together?"[109] Although many nonbelievers cite her brother's significant involvement as a way to undermine her artistic agency, this intimate songwriting process is quite the anomaly in commercial music, where widely circulated demo tracks and co-writer counts in the dozens are routine, if not requisite.

Eilish and O'Connell have continuously attempted to defend the sincerity and posterity of their work by ensuring the general public that they care immensely about their craft.

---

107 Bain, "A Day in the Life," *LNWY.*

108 Tim Ingham, "'Once You Help an Artist Build a Robust Business, a Lot Starts to Happen for Them'," *Music Business Worldwide,* March 31, 2020.

109 Joe Coscarelli, "Watch Billie Eilish and Her Family Talk About How They Make Music | Diary of a Song," *The New York Times,* uploaded on April 1, 2019, YouTube video, 8:02.

They insist that they utilize their extensive training in music composition to inform their artistic decisions. O'Connell has taken it upon himself to publicly defend his sibling's artistic honor, drawing a schematic parallel to a notorious musicological controversy from back in the early seventeenth century, when Giulio Cesare Monteverdi defended his composer brother Claudio Monteverdi against the harsh critiques of fellow composer Giovanni Maria Artusi. Over the course of a fervent debate, the Monteverdis asserted that for every old, established practice, a new, dissimilar practice can be generated and still be of quality. Defensively, Claudio Monteverdi stood up for his own artistic integrity: "I do not do things by chance … have faith that the modern composer builds on foundations of truth."[110]

In an April 2019 episode of "Diary of a Song," a popular periodic video series hosted by *The New York Times'* Joe Coscarelli, the duo makes a similar case for the value of Eilish's music. Outlining their creative process, Eilish and O'Connell detail how they see each song they write as an opportunity to inhabit a character and generate a work of realistic fiction.

On "bury a friend," a nightmarish pseudo-nursery rhyme, Eilish and O'Connell recall generating the shuffle beat that pulsates throughout the track, which O'Connell hoped would engage a large audience: "It feels kind of like a football chant … a body-friendly rhythm."[111] Less easily digestible is the song's structure, which starkly deviates from the radio standard

---

110 Denis Arnold and Nigel Fortune, *The Monteverdi Companion* (New York: W.W. Norton & Company, 1968), 159.

111 Coscarelli, "Diary of a Song," YouTube video.

(verse, chorus, verse, chorus, bridge, chorus), instead taking on the progression of hook, verse, pre-chorus, drop, hook, verse, alternate verse, bridge, pre-chorus, drop, hook. The synthetic stems in the song borrow from quotidian noises that Eilish has come across, including sounds of a dentist's drill, a stapler, someone stepping on glass, and an easy bake oven timer.[112] Such eccentric samples may be anathema to musical pioneers of the past, but they are perfectly palatable to the outlandish tastebuds of a generation that has grown up glued to the chaos of Vine and TikTok.

These bizarre sonic strains highlight the intractability of Eilish's genre categorization. Publicly, she claims that one of her ultimate priorities is to forsake any labels that are assigned to her altogether: "I don't wanna be in the pop world, I don't wanna be in the alternative world, or the hip hop world, or the R&B world or, whatever the f*** music, you know—I want it to be, like, Billie Eilish music, you know, like, the *other* kind."[113]

On one hand, the ambiguity of Eilish's musical identity is an affront to the very idea of genre categorization, proving that one does not need to fit into a clear-cut box to succeed commercially. On the other hand, her trajectory may not be as wholly unprecedented as she claims or would like to believe. Although she is principally influenced by hip hop artists like Tyler, the Creator when it comes to production, she leans toward catchy refrains in the vein of contemporaries like Ariana Grande. Even still, her whispery vocals and

---

112 Ibid.

113 Ibid.

macabre lyrical choices secure her position in a lineage of alternative trailblazers such as Lana Del Rey, Grimes, and perhaps most notably, Lorde, whose adolescent disruption of the commercial music airwaves in the mid-2010s mirrors Eilish's path. When I first heard Eilish's music, I was instantly reminded of what it felt like to ruminate in Lorde's debut EP, *The Love Club*, as a sophomore in high school. Both artists radiate an ambiance of introspective angst, cultural cynicism, and emotional consciousness in their songs that belie—or, perhaps, affirm—their youthfulness.[114]

Though Eilish may not view herself as a pop star, the teams enveloping her certainly do. Interscope Records' rollout of her music has packaged and positioned her as the newest iteration of pop paramountcy as we stereotypically understand it. Certainly, her marketing strategy has drawn from the hip-hop apparatus in more ways than many pop stars of the past (for one, she dropped a series of singles and an EP across a three-year period before even launching an album instead of leading with a full-fledged project). That being said, the high production value of her public presentation has obfuscated her decidedly lo-fi music-making process.[115]

In another feature for *The New York Times,* critic Joe Coscarelli notes how her influential managers seemed to be beyond optimistic about her inevitable global domination during the initial phases of her career: "To speak to her business team and label bosses is to hear the phrase 'the biggest

---

114 Jonah Weiner, "Lorde's Teenage Dream," *Rolling Stone,* October 28, 2013.

115 Anne Steele, "Billie Eilish Has No Major Radio Hits. But She Does Have the No. 1 Album," *The Wall Street Journal,* April 9, 2019.

artist in the world' repeatedly, and in earnest, as a near-term goal. ... 'I do not see a ceiling,' said Brandon Goodman, one of Eilish's managers."[116]

The global scale of Eilish's branding and distribution strategy, and the confidence with which the bureaucratic forces that stand to benefit from her achievements have promoted her, have conjured up concerns. Can Eilish's success truly be ascribed to her sovereign creativity or to the cyclical authoritative power of the institutions who support her?

As explicated by David Suisman in 2009's *Selling Sounds*, the commercialization of the music industry since the twentieth century has meant that the "control of the acoustic environment—the 'soundscape'—[is] an issue with real social and political consequences," making way for a landscape in which "Much [depends] on which sounds the music industry [promotes] and which it [ignores] or [suppresses]."[117]

Having been backed by entities such as Interscope and Apple Music since 2016, when she was just fourteen years old, Eilish has had access to an abundance of opportunities to garner hype, build exposure, and craft a brand persona that she likely would not have managed to generate entirely on her own. Undeniably, she has benefited from the formulaic "promotion of some music—that of the music industry—over other music," contradicting the layer of exceptionalism that is often associated with her origin story.[118] In the eyes of

---

116 Coscarelli, "Not Your Typical 17-Year-Old," *The New York Times*.
117 Suisman, *Selling Sounds*, 13.
118 Suisman, *Selling Sounds*, 14.

many, Eilish's longstanding relationships with commercial entities have undermined her claim to artistic recognition.

Many young listeners, including some of my most music-obsessed friends, believe that the mania that surrounds Eilish has been imposed on them by advertising and media organizations, unwarranted by her abilities. Online music communities on platforms such as Reddit are abundant with representative samples of the type of gripes that Eilish incites: "The fact that she was practically unheard of until her first single, that somehow got a lot of streams, seems way too sketchy for me," muses Raxil10 on a forum in February 2019.[119] Another user, willmaster123, echoes these sentiments in his reply, claiming he "saw ads for her on Facebook like MONTHS before she ever blew up. Probably rich parents paying to promote her music."[120]

Many take issue with her designation as a pioneer, like user JohnCdf, who believes she is "over-sensationalized with headings like '16 year old Pop Prodigy'…she's a generic sixteen year old with enough production to put out her generic s-a-d trap."[121] Others claim she receives excessive credit for being hands-on, when in reality, her brother is the primary artistic force on her records: "The production by her brother is what really draws me to her music and what makes it unique in my opinion," says Maybe__llamas.[122]

---

119 Ghdust2, "Let's Talk: Billie Eilish," *Reddit*.

120 Ibid.

121 LovingYouNowJake, "Billie Eilish Is Overrated and Kind of Annoying," *Reddit*.

122 Ibid.

Regular listeners are not the only ones who maintain that the grand praise that Eilish has been receiving might be unwarranted, or at the very least, overstated. Columnist M.H. of *The Economist* points out that although Eilish is "a very modern kind of pop star" and a veritable "product of the internet," she is also "someone who's been carefully nurtured by the big corporations," having "[embraced] the benefits of the multinationals" since the start of her career. Ever paradoxical, Eilish "has employed both the new model and the old model," targeting both traditional gatekeepers and young fans directly on social media.[123]

One of the most damaging arguments against Eilish and her public image is the claim that she exploits mental health issues by incorporating themes of teenage depression and anxiety into her musical and visual aesthetic. In a scathing review of her album in April 2019, *Mother Jones* reporter Sam Van Pykeren denounces Eilish's inclination to glorify suicidal thoughts under the guise of supposed edginess and gimmicky sonic tricks. "Rather than wrestling with the intense and existential hopelessness of wishing to take your own life, Eilish opts to romanticize it," he laments. Scornful, he compares Eilish's lyricism to an "utterly oblivious Tumblr post." He dismisses her craft as juvenile, time-specific, and trivial, while also criticizing how her pop-friendly image has been deceptively presented to the world. To him, her album is nothing more than "an empty, even insulting, product…evidence of what pop music sounds like in the hands of a stereotypical gen-Zer."[124]

---

123 M.H., "Is Billie Eilish Really Changing Pop Stardom?" *The Economist*, April 05, 2019.

124 Sam Van Pykeren, "Billie Eilish's Mouthful of an Album Is an Overdramatic Tumblr Post Brought to Life," *Mother Jones,* April 5, 2019.

* * *

Analyzed daily by thousands of digital spectators, Eilish fails to meet every expectation that the public erects for a musician who is constantly glorified by the music industry and its media counterparts. But what many of Eilish's detractors neglect to consider is that institutions have determined which music is magnified, and which is not, even dating back to the coordinated diffusion of the Roman chant in the Frankish Lands in eighth-century Europe.[125] Such power dynamics have undoubtedly oscillated across disparate epochs, but they have remained schematically consistent; institutions have long prioritized certain music in the pursuit of social order and control.

Why, then, should Eilish, in her first years of adulthood, bear the brunt of the criticism for a phenomenon that has more or less *always* framed music consumption?

Maybe, to an extent, she was indeed "planted" by the industry—but that is not to say that the garden she has grown should be discredited. It is worth considering that Eilish did not race to the top because of a one-off, meme-able moment, or a days-long viral story, or even a single standout radio hit. Instead, she has sustained a thriving fan base that recognizes her for who she is as opposed to snippets of what she's done. She has garnered the kind of fan loyalty that leads to veritable longevity. Sure, seeds have been planted in her favor, but she has nurtured them to astounding avail.

---

125 Richard Taruskin, *The Oxford History of Western Music* (Oxford: Oxford University Press, 2010), 4.

In some ways, Eilish is "an avatar of a swift microgenerational shift," an identity that has made her "a hero to her peers and younger admirers, a high school cohort that seems more fiercely open about sadness, suffering, and sexuality than ever," as described by *Slate Magazine's* Carl Wilson in a 2019 review.[126] Her proximity in age to a huge portion of her fanbase has allowed her to cultivate a hyper-specific visual aesthetic alongside her daring musical choices: "performatively dead eyes (bored, at best), hair dyed in shades of electric blue and pale purple, an all-baggy anti-silhouette—a collective middle finger to the strictures of teen-pop sex appeal."[127] Eilish differs from her contemporaries in her defiant choice to "wear big, baggy clothes. Nobody can have an opinion because they haven't seen what's underneath. ... I never want the world to know everything about me."[128]

If figurative industry puppet masters truly have been sitting in boardrooms and hand-picking who to advance to the top of the charts on a whim (if only it were that simple), I'm relieved that they have chosen someone who represents genuine musical talent, social awareness, and unapologetic individuality. A fierce advocate for climate justice, Eilish has insisted that all of her upcoming world tours be conducted in as eco-friendly a manner as possible, just one social issue of many that she has publicly endorsed.[129] Although she is

---

126 Carl Wilson, "Billie Eilish's Debut Announces the Arrival of a New Kind of Teen Pop Star," *Slate Magazine,* March 29, 2019.

127 Coscarelli, "Not Your Typical 17-Year-Old," *The New York Times.*

128 Katrina Nattress, "Billie Eilish Explains Why She Wears Baggy Clothes in New Calvin Klein Ad," *iHeartRadio,* May 9, 2019.

129 Nick Reilly, "Billie Eilish Reveals Plans for Eco-friendly World Tour," *NME,* September 30, 2019.

just four years younger than I am, she makes me optimistic about the generation whose ethos she has helped establish.

Perhaps the most urgent issue at hand is not if Eilish is complicit in the institutional control of music, but for us, as listeners and tastemakers, to question how much that notion truly matters in the first place. Let us rethink where we are directing our blame and our scrutiny. Perhaps it is the institutions themselves we should be targeting and deconstructing, as opposed to their individual subsidiaries. Perhaps, we should also consider why we are so inclined to deride female "pop" artists for lacking creative agency, seeming to constantly search for opportunities to attribute their success to the powerful men who support them, while male artists and businessmen are disproportionately given credit for their achievements.

Are we weary of teenage girls who assume more power than suits our societal comfort? Are we unable to acknowledge that Eilish might have more to contribute than the agendas of the people who assist her?

In a September 2020 virtual interview with the Grammy Museum, Eilish reflects on the downsides of her rapid ascension: "I love the Grammys so much, but to be sitting in a room full of [my] idols and have them lowkey resent [me] … and then having those people's entire fandoms that I've been a part of for years, hate me … was very upsetting for me."[130]

---

130 Pop Base (@PopBase), "Billie Eilish on her Grammy wins: "I love the Grammys so much but to be sitting in a room full of your idols and have them lowkey resent you was very upsetting for me and then having those people's entire fandoms that I've been a part of for years, hate me," Twitter, September 17, 2020, 2:28 p.m.

Eilish may be straddling overexposure and underappreciation, a tension that contributes to her confounding identity.

When reporter after reporter tells us that she "insists on near-complete control," perhaps we ought to believe it. "Everything could be easier if I wanted it to," she tells *The New York Times*, "but I'm not that kind of person and I'm not that kind of artist. And I'd rather die than be that kind of artist."[131]

A young adult navigating the same confusing maze as the rest of us, Eilish is imperfect. Some of her choices, independently driven or guided by institutions, do indeed perpetuate harmful stereotypes. Furthermore, it might be true that her assumption of such a large portion of the figurative pie of success in music suppresses the ability of truly independent artists to snag a slice of their own. But perhaps, her keen understanding of the importance of marketing, playing the game, and garnering institutional validation is not an indication of her selling out or being exploitative as much as it is a clue to just how well she understands the musical landscape she is becoming a part of and enhancing. Perhaps, we should simply cut her a break!

At the end of the day, the enigmatic Eilish still has us talking and debating, with years ahead of her to prove us wrong— there is something rock n' roll about that. Undeniably, we will all pay attention to her future.

---

131 Coscarelli, "Not Your Typical 17-Year-Old," *The New York Times*.

K-POP THE POLYLITH

Cultural Empathy through Commercial Escapism

In June 2018, *Digital Music News* published an article with a bold premise: "Can We Stop Pretending K-pop is Popular?"[132] Some headlines explode like dynamite for years after they are published, while others age about as well as an ice cream cone under stage lights. An emblem of the latter scenario, what might have once been a permissible title for a think-piece has now become a laughably outdated conjecture.

In the sure-to-be roaring 2020s, it is ludicrous for anyone with a musical pulse to deny that the K-pop apparatus has achieved cultural ubiquity on a global scale—no pretending necessary. Once perceived as a niche fixture relegated to subcultural markets, K-pop has shape-shifted into a definitive pillar of the commercial music landscape, its inclination for innovation intensifying by the day.

"K-pop has swiftly become South Korea's number one cultural export," explain co-authors Maari Hinsberg and Claudia

---

132 Adam Buckley, "Can We Stop Pretending K-Pop Is Popular?" *Digital Music News*, June 21, 2018.

Vagle in an October 2019 report for Estonia's International Centre for Defence and Security.[133] In addition to domestic domination, BTS, the flagship of the K-pop revolution by virtue of their unrivaled accolades, has defied snickers and side-eyes by becoming a Grammy-nominated global behemoth, boasting multiple number-one albums on the *Billboard* 200 Albums Chart, a number one single on the *Billboard* Hot 100, and critical recognition stateside and beyond.[134]

As valuable to the economy as many multinational corporations, "BTS, alone contributed 3.6 billion dollars to [South Korea's] GDP [in 2018]," as per the Estonian ICDS.[135] The geographical source of this staggering statistic is telling; when a phenomenon is being critically dissected by a think-tank in a research hub five thousand miles away from its country of origin, we can be certain that it is internationally consequential.

When I was a middle schooler in West Los Angeles, a handful of my closest friends were principally defined by their identities as K-pop devotees. Although only some of them were of South Korean origin, all of them were fiercely dedicated to the cause. I'd walk into the library to review my algebra homework after my lunch period, eager for catch-ups and conversations to distract me from determining slopes, only to be overshadowed by the launches of the latest big-budget music videos from my friends' points of fixation—sometimes

---

133 Claudia Valge and Maari Hinsberg, "The Capitalist Control of K-pop: The Idol as a Product," *International Centre for Defence and Security,"* October 2, 2019.

134 Bryan Rolli, "BTS's 'BE' Debut Is Going to Be Huge—But Just How Huge?" *Forbes,* October 8, 2020.

135 Valge and Hinsberg, *International Centre for Defence and Security.*

2NE1's irreverent pop-rap hooks, other times Big Bang's flirtations with R&B. Perhaps most notably, PSY, whose zany visual for "Gangnam Style" is notorious for pioneering our contemporary conceptions of virality, sent shockwaves into my social circles and Facebook group chats as the first artist in the history of the internet to ever surpass one billion views on a music video.[136]

At the time, I was agnostic, like many members of the Western music ecosystem. I was capable of admiring this culture's colorful and unwaveringly buoyant iconography on a surface level but remained dubious of its outwardly overproduced (and by extension, overly corporate) sheen. The playground of K-pop was a happy-go-lucky haven—or perhaps, a decked-out shopping mall—for an audience that I didn't necessarily belong to. I was content to be excluded from the conversation, and I, in turn, excluded most of K-pop's biggest hits from my playlists. Back then, Top Forty radio in the United States certainly wasn't instructing me to do otherwise.

Meanwhile, my close confidants were harvesting their senses of self by engaging with this music. One of my dearest friends from school, Francesca Walker, moved to New York at the same time as I did to study English at Columbia University. Having grown up near Los Angeles' Koreatown, she was first introduced to this music by local friends who inducted her into their obsession. Today, she cherishes the fact that she could rely on K-pop as the daily soundtrack to her tempestuous teenage years.

---

136 William Gruger, "PSY's 'Gangnam Style' Hits 1 Billion Views on YouTube," *Billboard*, January 21, 2012.

"I had a really difficult time in high school," she recalls during our Zoom heart-to-heart, donning her signature septum piercing and silver rings to match. "I remember there was one night when my favorite uncle had passed away. My mom was absolutely devastated. And me, having weird brain chemistry, and not understanding anything going on with myself ... I didn't really know how to cope. I didn't want to feel that sadness in that moment, so I watched a Girls Generation video. The brightness of the colors, and the fashion, and the outfits—it all seemed very outlandish to me, just overblown, oversaturated, fifty million genres distilled into one three-minute and fifteen-second song. But that stimulation was really exciting," she explains, as if recounting a fable.

"It's just happy! It's stuff that makes me feel happy. And I've learned to not be ashamed of listening to stuff that just makes me feel happy. It was what I needed during those really difficult parts of my life. Going home and being able to sit in my room and watch videos of my favorite artists was really the highlight of my day, every day."

The emotional exchange between K-pop fans and their favorite artists and bands is routinely represented by Western media sources and music communities as inherently transactional, devoid of personal significance. In a class I took during the fall semester of my senior year in college, my music business professor raised concerns about supporting a musical realm that operated by what she deemed were questionable ethical parameters. "It's just kind of creepy," she whispered to our class, citing the robotic precision of K-pop's signature choreographic styles—and the cunning of the business teams who propelled it.

On some level, her claims were not unfounded. There are elements of the so-called K-pop machine that are ostensibly nefarious. The corporations in charge of developing and managing K-pop idols have long been criticized for the restrictions they enforce regarding artists' autonomy. They closely patrol their most crucial creators and their every move to suppress artistic democratization. In the aforementioned report from Estonia's ICDS, Hinsberg and Vagle cite latent cultural appropriation, contractual slavery, and physical and sexual violence as just a few of the harmful strains that are perpetuated by the teams behind K-pop.[137]

But Francesca attributes much of the widespread resistance of K-pop to ethnocentrism, informed by her identity as a Black woman regularly traversing predominantly white or otherwise non-Black spaces. "The criticisms that I've heard of K-pop from people that never listened to it weren't based on any of the real issues that were facing artists there. It was always about the men looking hyper-feminine and everybody looking the same. It seems to be very set in stereotypes that we have about East Asian people: them not being discernibly different from each other, them not being masculine," she posits.

Whatever "it" that my teacher was alluding to when referencing K-pop is intractable. When I spoke to Wooseok Ki, a law student at the University of Pennsylvania and the author of *K-POP: The Odyssey*, a guidebook meant to serve as a written counterpart to K-pop's abundance of audiovisual content, he was insistent on dismantling the notion that K-pop can

---

[137] Valge and Hinsberg, *International Centre for Defence and Security*.

be essentialized down to a single word or phrase. In fact, he hesitates to even categorize it as *just* a genre, or *just* an aesthetic movement, or *just* a regional designation. At best, it can be classified as an amorphous cultural phenomenon that indicates different meanings to different parties, largely dependent on perspective and agenda: "Western media has this tendency to group K-pop communities as a monolith, but 'the K-pop fandom' doesn't really exist. There's no one group to unite everyone."

Artists too, are often categorized by Western spectators as "factory girls or robots on a conveyor belt, as if companies pump out idols." Ki agrees that K-pop companies do indeed systematize the artist development process, but he questions whether they deserve to be singled out for spearheading such a practice: "ultimately, entertainment is a cultural product. I think people forget to realize that the artists that you see in the Western setting, like Travis Scott, are just as manufactured. For some reason, when they talk about K-pop, everything is portrayed as mechanized. But there's a symbiotic bond between the artists and the fan culture that creates a special kind of effect."

Francesca, too, wonders if K-pop's detractors are dismissing it without paying mind to its nuances. "I would just hope that if people said 'I don't like K-pop'—which is a really difficult statement to make, because K-pop is a whole umbrella of hip-hop artists, and R&B artists and straight bubblegum pop singers—it's not purely because of some weird visual, aesthetic, xenophobia," she notes. "That, I think, is unfair."

In the years since *Digital Music News* dared to doubt the commercial potency of K-pop, discourse surrounding the phenomenon—and my understanding of it—has evolved as a result of its accelerated infusion into American culture. I've heard "Boy with Luv," BTS' collaboration with American pop staple Halsey, in more Manhattan Starbucks' than I can count. Because of my College Marketing role at Sony Music's distribution wing, The Orchard, I've now promoted several K-pop campaigns bolstered by industry giants such as JYP Entertainment and, most notably, Big Hit Entertainment, the South Korean entertainment and content tycoon that runs BTS' behind the scenes.

Whatever these companies are selling, people around the world are buying, and perhaps not as passive pawns. K-pop fans "take an active, participatory role in their consumerism," asserts Maria Sherman, a cultural critic and the author of *Larger Than Life: A History of Boy Bands from NKOTB to BTS* in a June 2020 conversation with *The New Yorker's* Amanda Petrusich. The notion that "every boy band or girl group" and its fanbase "is frivolous, manufactured" and "unserious" underplays the veritably emotional position that K-pop artists assume in their fans' lives.

Furthermore, beyond serving as active consumers and decision makers, K-pop stans wield the caliber to harness their monumental cyber influence to highlight pertinent social issues. During the June 2020 resurgence of the Black Lives Matter movement, K-pop fanbases flooded racially offensive hashtags, such as #WhiteLivesMatter, across social media platforms. Sharing copious amounts of video clips of their favorite idols, they overpowered voices of hatred and exemplified the progressive power of online fan culture, a realm that is often deemed untamable.[138]

---

138 Amanda Petrusich, "K-Pop Fans Defuse Racist Hashtags," *The New Yorker,* June 5, 2020.

At the top of my final semester of college, I finally had the chance to experience this fanaticism firsthand. As soon as my boss asked me to attend a Stray Kids concert at the Hulu Theater at Madison Square Garden and to capture my experience on social media, I texted Francesca, imploring her to come along as my plus one—she obliged, with strings of wide-smiled emojis and recommendations of tracks to explore in advance of the show.

Leading up to the night of the concert, I was awestruck by the pervasiveness and precision of the group's fans—labeled affectionately by the band as "Stay"—on social media. Every time I unleashed a promotional post into the feed, they reacted as if I had agreed to proselytize their religion, tagging their friends, reposting my content, and cultivating a sense of perpetual togetherness, mobilized around this music. "What I love most about K-pop fandoms is that they're protective of the groups that they love, but they want everybody to love them," Francesca tells me. "They don't want it to be an exclusive thing where only a few people listen to it. They get really excited when people show interest, genuine interest, no condescension, no patronization, just genuine interest. They want to share that with people. And I think that that's beautiful and great," she says, "because it totally lacks pretension."

More curious than ever, I perused a handful of Stray Kids' cinematic music videos in preparation for the concert. Although they were unlike anything I would have ever sought out in my spare time, the sheer grandeur of it all—of every group member's gold-plated collar and every fan's in-group, inside-joke-equipped musing in the comments section—was impossible not to admire in its intensity.

We arrived at The Garden thirty minutes past showtime, on the same night as a Knicks game. Our haphazard twists and turns in the grand concourse and vacant stares of perplexion revealed our objective before we could seek out a map. "You here for Stray Kids?" a security guard asked us, snickering. Was it that obvious? She directed us up a series of newly renovated escalators, and we barreled into the auditorium's audiovisual whirlpool.

Concerts rarely abide by the timestamps on their corresponding tickets, but Stray Kids strayed from this cliché, attuned to the fact that many of their fans have strict bedtimes. We squeezed our way past aisles of collective hyperventilation as a video interlude flashed across the screens in front of us, mocking our lack of punctuality. By the time we reached our seats, all eight members of the band stood aligned on stage, skin glistening under blood red strobe lights, their black mesh bodysuits synchronized thread by thread, ready for showtime.

Equally stimulated by the chorus of adolescent screams and the trap-infused pop beats that were roaring out of the speakers in front of us, I soon found myself swept away in the spectacle. At first, I filmed some videos "for work content," but eventually, I realized that this was worth documenting for my personal stash of souvenirs. By the time the second choruses of the group's biggest hits came around, I had already caught onto their irresistible melodies, able to reproduce them like any superfan in my vicinity could. Often conjured up in labs by analytical producers with arrays of era-specific musical trends in their arsenal, these globally oriented bangers are explicitly—and subliminally—infectious.

It was only when a middle-aged woman tapped me on my left shoulder that I reclaimed my footing in reality. "Excuse me, could you please sit down? My kid can't see." Of course, as soon as I realized that I, a twenty-one-year-old man, was blocking the view of a seven-year-old girl who was probably experiencing the most intense dopamine rush of her life thus far, I sank into my seat without protest. But I couldn't help but smile to myself about the fact that I had been led to let loose, even for a moment, leaving most of my skepticism at the door.

The concert contained not one millisecond of inactivity, not one chance to catch your breath—not that anyone in the crowd was in demand of one. In between performances, massive screens, some centered on the stage, others flanking it on either side, entertained fans with trivia questions, dance tutorials, and atmospheric interludes, often tentpoled by the group's self-fulfilling slogan: "Stray Kids everywhere, all around the world!"

"You don't understand how immersive and overwhelming of an experience K-pop is until you go to a concert," insists Francesca. "It's moving, being in a sea of fans all chanting the words to a song in a language that they probably don't even speak." When members of the group took pauses in between dance routines to address their audience, some more well-versed in English than their colleagues, they adopted a confessional tone, outlining their backstory and riffing off of the adrenaline-infused emotional investment of their fans.

Throughout the show, a pesky voice inside my head reminded me that all of these pleas for engagement were ultimately gimmicks, meticulously orchestrated marketing tools designed to catalyze consumption. But perhaps, that is not a justification for sheer denouncement. I enjoyed succumbing to the fantasy, escaping into this ether of excitement. "People always act like we're participating in some sort of bacchanalian revelry," Francesca jokes, but "I know that at its best, K-pop has always been a space where I could find people that had such intense passion and love and just wanted to share that with others." Others, like me.

As we danced, I was reminded of my days at Disneyland. Sure, you know that it's a corporate behemoth—but there's still value in holding tightly onto the idea that it's just your personal wonderland. K-pop creates space for this sensation with more finesse than any American act I've ever witnessed; as *Forbes*' entertainment contributor Bryan Rolli puts it in his September 2020 article, "they just beat other artists at their own game."[139]

Suspending disbelief is a thrill, even if it conceals the throes of commercialism. Consuming colorful content can be, at best, liberating, and at worst, a temporary boost of happiness. That bet seems safe enough to me.

Furthermore, it's always edifying to have experiences that are so undeniably energizing that we are forced to strip ourselves of the cultural biases that have defined our frameworks of taste since childhood, whether we've noticed them or not. K-pop's diffusion in America has the capacity to confront some of the most nefarious normative standards regarding

---

[139] Bryan Rolli, "BTS Didn't 'Cheat' Their Way to No. 1 on the Hot 100. They Just Beat Other Artists at Their Own Game," *Forbes*, September 28, 2020.

masculinity and beauty standards that plague the Western outlook. Seeing a boy with pink hair and a perfectly contoured face being heralded as a teen heartthrob felt, to me, like an uplifting sign of societal progress.

As the house lights switched back on and we began to shuffle our way out of the venue (at 10:30 PM sharp), the sugar high of childlike fanaticism and performative excess faded away. I began to worry, again, about a system that so closely patrols and restricts its most crucial creators, while still presenting its final products in seemingly perfect and infinitely palatable packages to lure in would-be-fans, like myself.

Though my feelings about K-pop remain nebulous, one concert couldn't have ever given me a panoramic perspective, for there is so much more to this world than a single group on a single night with a single fanbase.

From a business perspective, the K-pop phenomenon's economic dominance legitimizes its commercial prowess with each new accolade. But it will take critical considerations from music's most prominent thinkers and executives to ensure that we respect these cultural developments while refraining from magnifying its most damaging elements. Crucially, K-pop deserves the same nuance of analysis that we afford so many of our favorite polylithic virtues and vices.

Even if a piece of art is not directed at us, it's possible to appreciate the value it might serve in someone else's life. Our own opinions of it, too, might evolve as we become further exposed to its true character. This is a mode of cultural empathy that we ought to flex more often, especially when it comes to something as emotionally and bodily penetrative as listening to music. "When something that is not your thing blows you away, that's one of the best things that can happen. It means you are something more and something other than you thought you were," explicates art critic Dave Hickey in his essay "Goodbye to Love."[140]

The fact that K-pop is popular is, at this point, unquestionable. But beyond that, it's also promising. K-pop is emblematic of the potential of a more globally synergistic, community-oriented, and exchange-prone music ecosystem. And ultimately, isn't that what all of us, devotees and detractors alike, should be striving for?

---

140 Dave Hickey, *Perfect Wave: More Essays on Art and Democracy* (Chicago: University of Chicago Press, 2017), 23.

JON & POP

Community Formation through Pop Music

Ah, pop music. As identifiable as the Mona Lisa, as accessible as a Big Mac, as fantastic as Hogwarts' Great Hall.

You're at a party. You're in the zone. You've successfully, albeit temporarily, eliminated the thought of Monday's impending essay from your brain. Suddenly, an unmistakable melody infiltrates the airwaves that envelope you.

Perhaps it's four iconic, synthesized, comfortingly clichéd chords: A minor, F major, C major, G major. Perhaps it's an artist's recognizable banter preceding a sonic storm. Or perhaps it's a vocal gymnastics routine that has been burned into the collective consciousness of your entire age group. This is the type of hit record that mobilizes everyone, if only momentarily.

The chorus hits. The whole room croons along. This communal dopamine exchange is euphoric, cultivated by the most historically effective stimulant of all. For three and a half minutes, you unite with your fellow listeners, belting out syllabic patterns you might not even be cognizant of, and somehow, by some magic, you forget about the divided world outside the door, dancing along to your favorite, classic, unmistakably pop, pop song.

To a generation of young adults whose every second is usurped by one newly implemented distraction after another, the simplicity of a memorable chorus and a four on the floor beat is a welcome source of comfort. But come tomorrow, when the 12:15 PM hangover and existential stress sets in, most of us will deny all association, shrugging off the fact that we successfully belted out every ad-lib in the bridge of vintage Ke$ha's' "Your Love Is My Drug" not ten hours prior. It was, of course, but a fleeting display of irony, we'll insist—for the sake of social self-preservation.

As a reluctantly bisexual middle schooler in a heteronormative hub of West Los Angeles, self-preservation was once my biggest concern. Can I "get" a girl, or do I like pop music? Am I cool, or do I like pop music? Do I have good taste, or do I like pop music? In eighth grade, after my first girlfriend broke up with me following four months of awkward movie dates, a boisterous classmate pulled me aside on the school bus: "Dude, quit listening to Gaga, and you'll be good to go." The whole bus cackled. Bile churned in my chest. Throughout my turbulent journey through adolescence, I swiftly perceived the ways in which notions of shame are embedded in the societal fabric of pop music's position in culture. For years following, I'd traverse music forums centered on pop music in incognito mode; I'd learned to hide, as have many devotees of pop. Except for Jon.

Jon is my best friend. And as a self-proclaimed pop music aficionado, he claims ownership over the vice he sees as a virtue. A typical text from Jon reads like a multidimensional, social-platform-surmounting, reference-ridden meme, a stirring symbolization of our chaotic media landscape that would send most consumerism-detesting anthropologists into a frustrated frenzy. Inevitably, such a text includes (1) keyboard vomit ("jnfjsjdmMzkgkkdmsmf), (2) absurdist punctuative enthusiasm (!!! ,, ...), and (3) emphatic extolment of one or more pop music icons ("I simply ... don't know a better person than Charli XCX").

Long before I became privy to his stylistic digital tendencies, I met Jon when we both studied away in Paris during our junior year of college. He introduced himself as a biology major with med-school aspirations who was on the swim team. He was nice enough, conversational enough; we initially connected over mutual friends, café cremes, saucisson-secs, and tepid group visits to the Louvre—predictable memories of circumstance. But what would ultimately bond us together more than any musée or meal, in a longstanding way, was our shared adoration of pop music.

The *lingua franca* of the pop music universe is encyclopedic cultural knowledge. Pop fans all know, for example, that Mariah "doesn't know" who JLo is.[141] We all know that when Gaga bled on stage during her landmark performance of "Paparazzi" at the 2009 MTV Video Music Awards, she was referencing the death of Princess Diana and the martyrdom

---

141 Marissa G. Muller, "Mariah Carey Finally Explains That Jennifer Lopez 'I Don't Know Her' Meme," *W Magazine*, November 28, 2018.

of fame.[142] We all know that the Ziggy Stardust era in the '70s was a demonstration of Bowie's love of acting and a keen desire to evade reality, not merely a marketing apparatus meant to generate shock value as perpetuated by the gnarly media, but a defiant artistic pursuit.[143] These are the mythic stories, of public figures with private intentions, that we were raised on and made to feel like we had singular access to. In the trenches of the pop stratosphere, you'll often hear references to "the general public," a cluster that is deemed entirely disparate from the veritable analysts, admirers, and arbiters of a genre that has historically been maligned. When we locate others who wield matching levels of worship, we hold on tight, and we can't, don't, won't let go.

On a Sunday one month into our semester abroad, Jon and I strolled by the Seine under a cotton-candy sunset, post charcuterie and pre-rosé, debating whether Ariana's enlisting of Pharrell as an executive producer on 2018's *Sweetener* had elevated or suppressed her artistic potential. As we agreed that it was a wholly positive thing that he had encouraged her to tap into the lower register of her vocal range and a wholly negative thing that he had lured her into a misguided, haphazard collaboration with Missy Elliott that even the most diehard fans struggled to appreciate, I bathed in the melancholy light of our unspoken kinship. This was someone who understood one of my fiercest passions. More so, this was someone who wouldn't shame me for loving something I had always been made to feel fundamentally misguided for loving.

---

142 Jocelyn Vena, "Lady Gaga Inspired by Princess Diana, Faith No More," *MTV*, September 2, 2009.

143 Jim Farber, "The Decade That Made David Bowie a Superstar," *TIME*, January 17, 2016.

For centuries, tastemakers have dismissed pop music as devoid of any real sense of artistic integrity or value in consuming. Music historian Richard Taruskin notes in *The Oxford History of Western Music* that as early as the fourteenth century, music aimed at a general audience was deemed tawdry, institutionally permitted solely to pacify its subjects and prevent potential rebellion, like some sort of sonic opiate. In 1300, Johannes de Grocheio, an urban magister at the University of Paris, introduced *Ars Musicae* into the artistic canon, a resonant sociological treatise that inextricably linked musical genres to class affiliations. Because of Grocheio's societal influence during this epoch, "Lower types of secular song, namely those with refrains" were perceived as "feasts of the vulgar," disparate from "complex" music targeting an intellectual and political elite. Such songs were meant to generate "low" or sensual pleasure, noted solely for their "utility in mitigating the sadness of human life and enabling men to bear their lot without protest … [serving an] … edifying purpose."[144]

Centuries later, German musicologist Theodor Adorno warned readers in his 1941 polemic "On Popular Music" that music designed for a mass audience incites a society of automatistic citizens, ambivalent and distracted, woefully susceptible to the manipulation of totalitarian forces.[145] Having been expelled by the Nazis from his position as a university instructor in Germany, Adorno raised concerns that the culture industry's inclination for standardization, namely in popular music, could facilitate totalitarian hegemony

---

144 Richard Taruskin, *The Oxford History of Western Music* (Oxford: Oxford University Press, 2010), 208.

145 Theodore A. Gracyk, "Adorno, Jazz, and the Aesthetics of Popular Music," *The Musical Quarterly* 76, no. 4 (1992): 526–42.

stateside as well.[146] This is a persistent narrative that we've all heard before, that to belt out Ke$ha while drunk at a club is to indulge in systemically-ordained Kool-Aid, ignoring our real problems in exchange for cheap nights of thoughtlessness. Pop music has long been denigrated for its associations with brainless imbibing.

The mass media revolution beginning in the twentieth century has only propagated such strains of institutional condemnation. In a 2017 analysis of pop music standom, Buzzfeed culture writer Pier Dominguez notes how "Labels like bobby-soxer, Beatlemaniac, or, in the case of Madonna's fans, 'wannabes' were all imposed on teenage white girls through the authority of straight white male critics, seeking to make sense of what appeared to be potentially disturbing outbursts of adolescent emotion and agency." Today, in quotidian digital life, "stans are still often portrayed in personal and psychological terms as potentially creepy or overinvested."[147]

Conventional understandings of a pop fan typically take the shape of one of two caricatures: Chris Crocker (of 2007's "Leave Britney Alone" fame), or Sophia Grace and Rosie (an excitable pair of pink-tutu-obsessed, British girl-bots who went viral in 2011 after covering Nicki Minaj's "Super Bass" and appearing on the Ellen Show).[148]

---

146 *Stanford Encyclopedia of Philosophy*, Winter 2015 ed., s.v. "Theodor W. Adorno," accessed October 14, 2020.

147 Alessa Dominguez, "Pop Music Stans Aren't Crazy, They're Having a Conversation," *Buzzfeed News*, September 21, 2017.

148 Allie Volpe, "'Leave Britney Alone': Chris Crocker 10 Years Later," *Rolling Stone*, September 13, 2017; Jazmine Gray, "Nicki Minaj, Sophia Grace and Rosie Return to 'Ellen'," *VIBE*, May 10, 2012.

Here lie our representative options: a crazed queer man who projects his melodramatics onto distant icons, or deluded flocks of pre-adolescent girls who aren't old or intelligent enough to distinguish sweet from saccharine. Either way, pop is abundantly attached to notions of wholly uncritical and juvenile consumption, as opposed to "disinterested" contemplation, a principle established by Immanuel Kant in 1790's *The Critique of Judgment,* as the optimal way to assert judgments about aesthetic beauty: from a distance, without bodily participation, and always with an aim to intellectualize.[149]

Despite my own affinity for pop, I too judged Jon for the extent of his devotion to the genre as our semester in Paris progressed. He was the first person I'd ever met who was emphatically proud of being a pop fan, who'd tell any new acquaintance how much the piercing jingle that played out of the Paris metro speakers when the doors opened reminded him melodically of the opening sequence of his favorite song, Carly Rae Jepsen's "Run Away with Me": "The intro to that song is a soaring saxophone solo, and it just kind of brings you in and immediately makes you feel good and excited and it pumps you up," he'd rave to me, and anyone who'd listen, with palpable fervor. I'd hear him, but I'd never quite listen, because subterraneously, I felt superior. The fact that I didn't *just* listen to pop music made me more valuable as a music percipient. Having studied classical music in the Eastern and Western traditions since my childhood, I understood that liking pop was not an identity worthy of openly donning. My shame concerning pop rendered my taste more permissible than his.

---

149 *Stanford Encyclopedia of Philosophy,* Spring 2019 ed., s.v. "Aesthetic Judgment," accessed October 14, 2020.

Certainly, tensions surrounding sexuality undergirded my resistance to Jon's degree of obsession. He's gay, "opening him up to the queer specificity ... of stan discussions," as illustrated by Buzzfeed's Dominguez.[150] On the other hand, as a bisexual man, once led to repress the side of myself I recognized as socially deviant, I never quite felt as though I had a right to carve out space in the world of pop standom. Not only did I simply not relate to or understand some of the typical preoccupations of many of my fanatic peers (I've never been, and probably never will be, a proponent of Britney Spears' musical talent or divine identity, for example), but the gendered environments that enveloped me growing up instructed me that this was a binary system, one that would one day require me to make tough choices. It has taken, and will continue to take, years of unlearning to bypass the biases society once promised were my only means of becoming socially viable.

Jon's memories of childhood as a pop fan prove far sweeter and more sentimental. "We grew up in that golden age of pop music—like the '90s and 2000s," he once told me. "Me and my mom would listen to Gwen Stefani all the time in the car." When he and I were growing up, "pop music," as lauded by superfans and as consumed by the general public, essentially referred to the same types of songs, as had been the case since the 1980s. For decades, what we now recognize as classic pop records dominated the soundscape, typically characterized by "simple lyrics, pleasingly generic production, and swelling, sugary hooks," as depicted by Buzzfeed's DJ Louie XIV. "Pop was an institution, the norm, the familiar as a style of music

---

150 Dominguez, *Buzzfeed News*.

and in who performed it, and it felt entrenched as America's most broadly enjoyed genre," he notes in an op-ed published in May 2019.[151]

As we navigate a new decade, however, pop music (the genre) is growing increasingly distinct from *popular* music (the descriptor of what is dominating the *Billboard* charts and Spotify stream counts). Each entails its own set of semi-tractable sonic elements and intricacies.

The contemporary dominance of the hip-hop genre, and a generational pushback against the very notion of genre categorizations, has forced "traditional" pop, which has become more of a homesick subcategory than a presiding umbrella term, to take a back seat in a streaming-driven ecosystem. These changes, according to *The New York Times*' Jon Caramanica, are the result of "the simultaneous triumph of several parallel sounds," including "punkish SoundCloud rap; bulbous Latin trap; chaotic K-pop; forward-thinking country music and more," a multicultural mélange of digitally catalyzed influences, sometimes essentialized as "Spotifycore."[152]

Of course, you'd be mistaken to believe that traditional pop has completely been erased from the airwaves in this process. During an email exchange, Jason Lipshutz, the Senior Director of Music at *Billboard Magazine*, assured me that there have been several "outliers like Jonas Brothers, Halsey and Shawn

---

151 DJ Louie XIV, "Carly Rae Jepsen and the Rise of the Micro Pop Star," *Buzzfeed News,* May 22, 2019.

152 Jon Caramanica, "How a New Kind of Pop Star Stormed 2018," *The New York Times,* December 20, 2018.

Mendes who have been able to shrug off that influence and find legitimate mainstream success."

However, as *The New York Times*' Caramanica explains, "they are effectively a niche proposition in the wider conversation."[153] Many seemingly infallible pop-cultural figures of yesteryear, who once filled pages of encyclopedic entries in the brains of fans like myself and Jon, have seen their crowds dwindle and their egos deflate, struggling to replicate or even marginally match up to their former cultural accolades. When was the last time you *witness*ed a new Katy Perry hit? Her last several singles have failed to even crack the *Billboard* Hot 100; she once tied Michael Jackson for the most number-one smashes from a single album.[154]

What happens when a genre with aesthetic elements that once originated out of an institutional desire to appeal to the masses no longer appeals to the masses? Interestingly, this evolution, which has deemphasized the commercial potency of pop music on a massive scale, has adorned the genre with a layer of subcultural legitimacy and critical acclaim that it has seldom been afforded historically. Take Kacey Musgraves, a primarily country songwriter with a notable pop tilt, whom mainstream radio largely ignored and scoffed at for her supposed commercial deficiency until 2018's *Golden Hour* won Album of the Year at the Grammys. Nobody was quite as taken aback as Musgraves herself, whose bewildered reaction, resembling a facial spasm, has become a meme amongst her

---

153 Caramanica, *The New York Times*.

154 Spencer Kornhaber, "How Pop Music's Teenage Dream Ended," *The Atlantic*, September 1, 2020.

small but relentlessly devoted flock of fans.[155] DJ Louie XIV labels Kacey a "micro pop-star," and someone like my friend Jon epitomizes her target audience.[156]

One night, near the end of our stay in the university housing complex in the fourteenth arrondissement we had been living in, we decided to get belligerently high via shitty Parisian joints with our friend Maddy, a transfer student from the University of Vermont who never quite understood why we city kids enjoyed pop music oh so much (she preferred her lane of indie-sentimentality à la Sleater-Kinney, Tennis, and Big Thief). Under a cloud-muffled moon, with all the lights switched off in my room, Jon decided that it was the perfect time of night to play us "Vroom Vroom," a track released by English singer-songwriter Charli XCX in 2016. Before he played the track, Maddy and I rolled our eyes in tandem—*what bubblegum-filler-mindless-uninspired-corporate-vulgar-march were we about to be subject to?*

To our surprise, the next three and a half minutes barreled us into a depraved but irresistible clownhouse-turned-discothèque on Halloween. The song, produced by experimental Scottish record producer SOPHIE, sounded nostalgic, structurally shaped like many pop classics (hook / verse / pre-chorus / chorus), and lyrically familiar (with hedonistic allusions to abundance, sex, and expensive cars, all fixtures in the pop lexicon). At the same time, the single was strikingly inventive, founded on a uniquely cacophonous

---

155 Cillea Houghton, "Kacey Musgraves' Reaction to Winning Grammy Album of the Year Is So Pure," *Taste of Country,* February 11, 2019.

156 DJ Louie XIV, *Buzzfeed News.*

rubber banded beat that resembled pots and pans clanging in a glitchy simulation. Schematically reminiscent of the internet subculture and musical style known as Vaporwave, this electronic music appropriated established musical clichés with frivol while complicating them with a sense of auditory unconventionality and futurism.

In 1944's *Dialectic of Enlightenment*, Adorno and his co-author Max Horkheimer snivel at the fact that "in light music the prepared ear can always guess the continuation after the first bars of a hit song and is gratified when it actually occurs"; however, in the case of "Vroom Vroom," I was primarily stirred by the juxtaposition—even dissonance—of the elements that I could indeed predict and the elements that took me entirely by surprise.[157] By reinventing institutionally originated aesthetic elements of pop music with singular layers of eccentricity, XCX reclaims her agency, transgressing expectations, including my own. Maybe it was the sativa, but I relished every second.

Upon "Vroom Vroom's" release three years ago, *Pitchfork* dismissed XCX's efforts as "pointedly uncommercial and abrasive."[158] Just a year later, the publication heralded her as "a vision of what pop music could be."[159] In 2019, Charli claimed a spot on *Pitchfork's* best of the decade list despite charting well outside of the US *Billboard* 200's top ten.[160] Lack of traditional commercial viability was once taken for granted as a categorical

---

157 Owen Hullat, "Against Guilty Pleasures: Adorno on the Crimes of Pop Culture," *Aeon*, February 20, 2018.

158 Laura Snapes, "Vroom Vroom EP," *Pitchfork*, March 23, 2016.

159 Meaghan Garvey, "Pop 2," *Pitchfork*, December 20, 2017.

160 Pitchfork, "The 200 Best Albums of the 2010s," *Pitchfork*, October 8, 2019.

pejorative in the pop world. Now, it is celebrated, a veritable realm of opportunity for the top of the "micro-pops."

In a June 2017 article, *NME* reporter Gary Ryan ponders the notion that "Pop music is escapism." "… At its best," he muses, "it suggests another way of life is possible."[161] The best pop music begs you to suspend disbelief, to dive into stories that are decidedly fictional. The best pop music invites its listeners into magical realms of simultaneous remembrance and imagining, to indulge and to invent all at once. Nobody understands, and has understood, this idea better than Jon. And while I always gave him credit for loving this type of music, it has taken me, and society, far too long to acknowledge the active self-awareness that its framework can entail.

Perhaps, to escape—in a club, in the car with your mom, or in conversation with your best friend—can be a fiercely creative mindset, a conscious choice to participate in a cultural narrative. Perhaps, it is not merely a mode of passive resignation that institutions coerce us into abiding by after all. Jon has been a mirror, not a lamp, reminding me that the degradation of pop music stems from the degradation of social groups who have been systematically minimized for seeking to indulge. But teenage girls and queer men are much more than just hapless consumers, easy to lure into vulgarity; they're craftsmen and community-builders too. It's about time we recognize them as such. Perhaps pop music is not against our better judgment; it *is* our better judgment.[162]

---

161 Gary Ryan, "Inside the 'One Love Manchester' Gig – What You Couldn't See on TV," *NME*, June 5, 2017.

162 James B. Twitchell, *Lead Us into Temptation: The Triumph of American Materialism* (New York: Columbia University Press, 1999), 20.

Pop music didn't suddenly become conceptual, meaningful, and artistic overnight because of a couple of glowing *Pitchfork* reviews and the overdue validation of the Recording Academy. But the rising reformulation of the genre as a newly respected artform becoming recognized in concentrated spaces is a promising development against a centuries-long lineage of denunciation.

The summer after our time in Paris, Jon brought me to a Carly Rae Jepsen concert in New York City. The energy in the sold-out Hammerstein Ballroom, which holds a moderate capacity of about 2,200 people, was infectiously buoyant; nearly every head in the room could belt out every word, to the obliviousness of the general public outside the venue doors. In an interview with *Elle Magazine's* Brennan Carley to celebrate the five-year anniversary of 2015's *Emotion*, now a bona fide cult classic in the pop canon, Jepsen embraces the evolving role of pop: "I was really searching for what sort of pop music was authentic and made sense to me. … And I think it's brought together a lot of really lovely humans. I'm so happy being one of the orchestrators of the night. … And I think that's the gift that's continued to give since *Emotion*, a feeling of total joy in these rooms—and safety."[163]

As Jon and I jumped up and down with each crashing chorus, melting into the fictions we'd reclaimed as our own, I thought about how the rapport we'd built resembled the kinship that members of older generations often romantically ascribe to

---

[163] Brennan Carley, "Carly Rae Jepsen Looks Back on Her Game-Changing Album E•MO•TION Five Years Later," *Elle,* September 2, 2020.

the subcultural, indie shows of their childhoods, a nostalgic relic come present reality.

Maybe pop music is not just the cathartic, drunken apex of a wild night out. Maybe it's the whole damn day, dawn, dusk, and Jon included.

SEIZING THE SUBJECTIVE
The Evolution of Music Criticism

"A critic is a person who encounters music, examines her responses, considers the context, and articulates whatever comes up during this process, whether it's desire, joy, anger, even repulsion. It's not a thumbs-up-or-down game..."
—ANN POWERS IN *SLATE MAGAZINE*[164]

Over the course of my college years, my understanding of the role of a critic has evolved from the image of an animated Anton Ego turning his nose up at a rodent chef in Pixar's *Ratatouille* to a stylish, culturally-savvy New Yorker scribbling notes in a moleskine notebook on the balcony of a buzzworthy concert.[165]

---

164 Ann Powers, "Entry 7: Fine, I'll Write About What Lana Del Rey Said About Me," *Slate Magazine*, December 19, 2019.

165 Emmet Asher-Perrin, "For Love of Art and the Education of a Critic: Ratatouille," *Tor.com*, June 18, 2012.

The final in-person event that I attended as an undergraduate was a symposium entitled "Journalism Under Pressure." Amanda Petrusich—my professor, a staff writer for *The New Yorker,* and my part-time personal superhero—asked me to co-moderate a panel of alumni critics with a fellow student. Preparing for this event was an honor that bookended my college experience. During my very first semester, I took Petrusich's introductory writing course, igniting my fascination with writing about music culture. Four years and several more writing courses later, I took her advanced seminar and worked alongside her on the panel, my appreciation for critics at record heights.

The panelists, former students who had gone on to write for publications such as the *Rolling Stone* and *Jezebel,* affirmed the notion that music journalism is, in fact, under immense pressure. As they spoke about their daily tasks, from synthesizing research, to demystifying cultural concepts, to interfacing with unpredictable artists, they noted how precarious their profession was. From the rock-climbing wall that is freelancing to the bureaucratic breeding ground that is the corporate media landscape, these digitally-oriented critics have not charted well-trodden career trajectories—and perhaps never will. Artists once relied on music journalists for press coverage during release cycles. Today, thanks to surges of surprise releases, social media countdowns, and Spotify banners, artists don't even seem to recognize the very premise of what a music critic is, ignorant of their value in the music ecosystem.

Long gone are the days during which radio jockeys and journalists were anointed by the public to wield the exclusive ability to determine which songs and stars were culturally relevant. Music listeners have more sovereignty than ever to choose which forms of art to actively engage in. The constantly developing digital contexts of the twenty-first century increasingly permit fans to communicate directly with one another and with the artists they admire, instead of subscribing to the musings of middlemen. With access to limitless opinions and rankings, from forums to comment sections to YouTube-broadcasted rants, why must a music fan rely on the cultural critic? What cultural capital could a critic even boast to impose his or her taste on a stranger? Furthermore, why should artists abide by the arbitrary standards of editorial voices that are losing their potency in the oversaturated attention economy?

It seems to me that the critics who prevail are the ones who go beyond just determining quality, a tradition that is outdated to a generation that is prone to question the authority of any cultural institution that purports to assert universal objectivity. Contemporarily, there is no single rubric that determines having a "good ear" or a "good eye," maybe not even a single reality we could all claim to belong to.

What allows the modern critic to succeed is a keen ability to transcend the value that an automated number on a scale could already provide. Maybe that means she incorporates philosophical concepts into her analysis. Maybe that means he dedicates paragraphs to divulging the political schema that surrounds a given work of art. Maybe it means they embrace the way their convergence of identities has shaped their perspective, offering reflections that are generative because they stem from an entirely singular viewpoint. Separating art from its societal environment, and from the lens through which it is being perceived, is counterproductive. Some layer of subjectivity, and by extension, politicization, is now essential to propel effective dialogue and discourse as a critic.

* * *

During its rudimentary phases, however, art criticism was a forum for elite aristocrats to systematize standards of aesthetics and form. Likely conceived alongside the origins of many artistic disciplines themselves, the practice was once reserved for the upper echelons of society, a means for the ruling class to educate within an insular community of wealth and power. Some historians argue that Pliny the Elder of the Roman Empire represents the earliest notable semblance of an art critic. In 77 AD's *Natural History*, he analyzes the development of Greek sculpture and painting, identifying creative techniques and patterns in an encyclopedic manner.[166] Examining the social, cultural, or political implications of his subjects was hardly his scholarly priority, nor did it have to be. As a pioneer of artistic documentation, even attempting to unravel the makeup of the artworks he analyzed on an aesthetic level was imaginative.

If we fast-forward to eighteenth-century Europe, we see that the fundamental principles that drive the profession of criticism have ostensibly remained intact. That being said, trailblazers such as France's Denis Diderot were able to disrupt longstanding traditions by championing their right to

---

166 Pliny the Elder, *The historie of the world : commonly called, The naturall historie of C. Plinius Secundus* (London: Adam Islip, 1634).

evaluate while simultaneously responding to the desires of the public—a public to whom art was newly attainable as entertainment in the form of salons and galleries, a facet of many people's daily lives. As illustrated by California-based art historian Thomas E. Crow, Diderot's assumption of art criticism "was on the heels of the first generation of professional writers who made it their business to offer descriptions and judgments of contemporary painting and sculpture. The demand for such commentary was a product of the similarly novel institution of regular, free, public exhibitions of the latest art."[167] The public, with newfound access to practices that were once withheld from them, primarily sought out aesthetic introductions and clarifications.

During the nineteenth and twentieth centuries, art critics around the world cultivated more caliber than ever to not only identify but also influence the proceedings of art creation. Critics propelled artistic movements in and out of trend, determining the cultural worth of certain modes of artistry. In the 1920s, the genre of jazz became an artistic and commercial phenomenon across the music ecosystem, at the same time as the institution of print journalism was flourishing. According to the historian Mary Herron Dupree, "the debate about Jazz—about its origins and defining characteristics ... was of paramount interest to those concerned with the present and future of American music and was waged with particular vigor in periodicals ... and among music journals."[168] The staggering amount of coverage centered

---

167 Thomas E. Crow, *Diderot on Art, Volume I: The Salon of 1765 and Notes on Painting* (New Haven: Yale University, 1995), x.

168 Mary Herron Dupree, "'Jazz,' the Critics, and American Art Music in the 1920s," *American Music* 4, no. 3 (1986): 287–301.

on jazz music simultaneously contributed to its proliferation and its corresponding air of contention. Debates surrounding its political implications, largely centered on race and class, became as commonplace as consumption of the genre itself.

During this golden age of journalism, artists still understood that approval from the most celebrated critics could carve out passageways to glory. Many readers, too, revered critics. Lacking access to disciplined perspectives on such subjects, they derived meaning from the words of wonder these journalists provided. It was under each critic's discretion to decide whether or not to focus on aesthetic analysis or political examination. Both were deemed acceptable, for critics were widely understood as trustworthy specialists. Audiences were beginning to actively engage with and respond to critical pieces, confined only by the one-sided nature of twentieth-century journalistic communication.

* * *

Today, the previously hierarchical division that once existed between the reader and the critic has all but dissolved. The very function of modern art criticism relies on engagement and exchange.

A 2016 Pew Research Center study emphasizes an unsurprising shift: 38 percent of adults who consume media do so digitally whereas only 20 percent do so through print media.[169] Two years later, the Center reported that social media in particular had outpaced print newspapers in the

---

169 "State of the News Media 2016," *Pew Research Center,* Edition 13 (2016): 45.

US as a news source.[170] Paradoxically, the rise of the internet and social media has simultaneously strengthened and diminished the value of criticism as a concept. On one hand, more of the general public has the opportunity to magnify their own critical perspectives, to be critics themselves. On the other hand, professional critics now find it exceedingly difficult to elevate their voices over all the new players who have entered the market.

In economic terms, what was once an oligopoly, entailing battles between the best pieces from the *Variety*s and *The New York Times*' of the world, has now become a monopolistic competition, ridden with 280-character think-pieces and self-published *Medium* op-eds, alongside every other conceivable form of digital entertainment. An individual critic can no longer take the public's respect for granted. Today, an uninformed Tweeter might command more attention than a degree-carrying reporter for a reputable magazine.

"These days, 'good taste' seems like a silly and old-fashioned idea," notes my former professor Amanda Petrusich in her February 2017 reflection on the Grammys in *The New Yorker*. "All taste is good taste; the heart wants what it wants; everything is permissible so long as it is inclusive."[171] At this point, a critic's purely aesthetic assessment of the quality of a piece of art would likely fall victim to noise-cancelling.

---

170 Elisa Shearer, "Social Media Outpaces Print Newspapers in the U.S. as a News Source," *Pew Research Center*, December 10, 2018.

171 Amanda Petrusich, "The 2017 Grammys Have No Answers," *The New Yorker*, February 13, 2017.

Furthermore, the internet promotes a culture that is obsessed with democratic mean. Sites such as Rotten Tomatoes and Metacritic, which aggregate scores, often serve as quantitative yardsticks for cultural consumers to direct the choices they make. Readers are more prone to reference numbers that have been curated algorithmically than full-fledged thoughts on a writer-by-writer basis. The success of such services can be attributed to the immense convenience that they promise; it is much easier to glance at a score momentarily than it is to invest in reading an individualized review. And if aesthetic excellence is but a subjective benchmark, why should the average reader yearn for advice from an alleged professional?

To Petrusich, political context—and embracing that very notion of inherent subjectivity—might just be the optimal asset. When I sat across from her in her cozy, pastel-hued office during the spring semester of my freshman year, just months after Donald Trump was elected president of the United States, we discussed the consequences and possibilities that emerge from "living in a hyper-politicized moment."

"It's a strange sort of transitional time in American politics. For the first time since we've been tracking these things, political editorials are as popular as entertainment stories. People are really hungry for that. Criticism that doesn't acknowledge the cultural moment and the reality of the way people live now and what's on people's minds and the fears that are being aggravated would seem kind of tone-deaf."

Petrusich engages readers by weaving in societal analysis into her examination of the sonic qualities of musical works: "We're no longer telling readers whether something is good or not. The readers have their own highly defined, singular taste. They can figure out what works for them, what they like. What the critic is there to do now is to maybe broaden your contextual understanding of something or broaden a creative understanding of something to point to bits that are interesting or to bits that echo something that came before or examine the kind of circumstances that led to the creation of the thing. It feels like people are really reading criticism carefully and responding to it. It feels like it's what people talk about on Twitter. It feels like it's part of the conversation."

In her review of Justin Timberlake's performance at the Academy Awards in 2017, Petrusich expands her discussion to pinpoint the corporate optimism present in American mainstream music in the wake of the presidential election.[172] In July 2020's "Why the Chicks Dropped Their 'Dixie,'" she interrogates the lineage of essentialist tropes in the country music ecosystem and their newly invigorated scrutiny in the era of cancel culture.[173] Petrusich's thousands of social followers are particularly drawn to this type of critical content, acutely attuned to political circumstances.

Perhaps we needn't glorify the eras during which aesthetic identification was the primary purpose of art criticism. Petrusich stresses how much she appreciates the evolving dynamic of the journalistic world: "Discussions of race, class, privilege—all that stuff is so important right now ... I'm always gonna lean toward tackling something in that way. In some

---

172 Amanda Petrusich, "Justin Timberlake Sells Optimism at the Oscars," *The New Yorker,* February 27, 2017.

173 Amanda Petrusich, "Why the Chicks Dropped Their 'Dixie'," *The New Yorker,* July 13, 2020.

ways, the critic's job has gotten harder, but I think it's better work. I think it's more fruitful and exciting work. I would rather do that work than just tell someone whether to buy something or not."

For the next generation of critics, political and perceptual considerations are primary colors on the palette, not just accent tones. Jenzia Burgos, a New York City-based writer and editor and my former classmate at NYU Gallatin, believes that her very identity as a working critic is a political act.

"I'm Latina. I grew up in the South Bronx," she tells me as we catch up over a Zoom call. "My whole life is an amalgamation of a lot of contexts, and the way I move through the world is very much colored by that background." In each of her pieces, whether published in *Pitchfork* or *Paste Magazine* or NYU Gallatin's array of publications during her time as a student, she believes it is crucial for her to embrace her subjectivities.

"I think that we are at a point in society where we don't *want* to engage with that context ... context of identity, context of nationality, context of sound ... because sometimes it's even easier not to. The main thing that I try to do is unearth as much of that information as possible because I think that it makes the experience of engaging with any art just that much richer."

While acknowledgment of societal context is integral to the agency of the modern critic, eloquent expression, too, might be worth prioritizing to the end of captivating an audience. Well-constructed critical pieces can metaphysically take on an artistry of their own, amplifying the intention behind the original artistic point of interest or even transcending it altogether. Critics who employ excellent writing techniques might solidify themselves as artists in their own right, differentiating themselves by virtue of their technique. Frank O'Hara, who lived in the mid-twentieth century, was famed for his poetry, curation, and criticism alike. He is primarily recognized as an original artist, as even his pieces of criticism were beautiful to engage with.[174]

"You know when you read an Amazon review and then you a read a professional book critic's review and you think, these are not the same; this thing is really elevating my view of this work and making me interrogate my own feelings about it and this other thing is just crazy," notes Petrusich. The right critic should be able to take on the "more important job than ever of separating the signal from the noise. I think there's already something to be said for a beautifully written thing. I want some craft in there!"

As technology develops, a critic's craftsmanship need not be limited to written pieces. In June 2020, during the resurgence of the Black Lives Matter movement following the murder of George Floyd and a wave of international protests, Burgos posted an informational Instagram photo series with a thought-provoking, feed-disrupting first slide: "Your favorite music exists because of Black people."[175] The ensuing photo album directed viewers to a meticulously-curated list of

---

174 Alina Cohen, "The Ongoing Influence of Frank O'Hara, the Art World's Favorite Poet," *Artsy,* April 3, 2018.

175 Jenzia Burgos (@jenziaburgos), 2020, "If you don't know the history of Black artists behind your favorite music, you don't really know your favorite music," Instagram photo, June 4, 2020.

articles written by critics documenting the Black origins of a wide range of genres, presented in striking shades of orange and white, sharable and distinctive.

Burgos' post was propelled by political frustration. Given her cultural background, she grew up privy to the Black origins of the genres she consumed, from rock to punk to hip-hop. During a phase when social media was oversaturated with content, ranging in usefulness and actionability, Burgos decided she could be most helpful by honing in on a subject that was relevant to her, one that she held unique expertise in. Donning her singular perspective, she welcomed everyone to the discussion instead of locking certain people out. Her post received upward of 150,000 likes, propelled by reshares from a long list of artists and music lovers, including Ariana Grande, the most followed woman on Instagram, two hundred million plus eyes on her every double tap. Burgos' following more than tripled in the ensuing weeks, rendering her as her own type of influencer—even artist, if you will.

Though disparate from Burgos, Anthony Fantano, the man *The New York Times*' Joe Coscarelli describes as "The Only Music Critic Who Matters (If You're Under 25)," also believes in inviting the public to join in on and contribute to his discussions, which usually take the form of conclusive and consistently-formatted YouTube reviews: "I had consciously chosen something that I found to be really uncomplicated because I envisioned the delivery and the makeup as being something that was easy to copy, so other people could get in on the conversation." Fantano's YouTube channel, *The Needle Drop*, boasts more than two million subscribers, having amassed six hundred million views since he joined the platform in January

2009. A commentator in and of the internet, sometimes perceived contemptuously by proponents of traditional media, he has ushered in a wave of similarly music-obsessed influencers across social media platforms: "What's most important to me is not the form that it takes, or the vehicle that it's being driven to me in, but really that it's observant, that it's passionate, and that the people who are doing it care."[176]

The future of music criticism is ambiguous. In October 2020, the parent companies of *Rolling Stone* and *Billboard* announced a joint venture, rendering the dwindling world of music media more consolidated than ever before. This partnership represented the latest in a long line of changes that has threatened the integrity of music journalism, as analyzed by *Pitchfork* editor Anna Gaca: "*The Fader* hasn't published an issue [in 2020]; *Q* closed this summer; *NME* ended its print edition in 2018, preceded by *Vibe* in 2014 and *Spin* in 2012; *Pitchfork* shuttered its specialty quarterly a few years ago; and *The Village Voice*, which helped establish music criticism as a staple of the alternative press, is long dead."[177]

But there are reasons to be optimistic, and resources to lead the way. Fantano, despite his polarizing position in the critical community, is committed to remaining independent, refusing to engage in contractual relationships with record labels and other music companies or potential buyers who seek to convolute his perspective.[178] Burgos plans to continue to harness her growing

---

176 Joe Coscarelli, "The Only Music Critic Who Matters (if You're Under 25)," *The New York Times*, September 30, 2020.

177 Anna Gaca, "What Does the Rolling Stone and Billboard Deal Mean for Music Fans?" *Pitchfork*, October 1, 2020.

178 Coscarelli, "Music Critic," *The New York Times*

social media following as a platform for her critical voice. In August 2020, she launched the Black Music History Library, an interactive and ever-growing website database containing over one thousand resources narrating the Black roots of popular and traditional music genres.[179] Moreover, she is considering spearheading a newsletter centered on music criticism to further educate her followers in as interactive a manner as possible. Evidently, despite having countless options at their fingertips, Burgos' audience is eager to listen to her clarifying words and insights, ready to revere a critic reimagining what it means to be a teacher with a helping hand—not just a keen eye and ear.

Technological innovations have endangered the dignity associated with being a critic by seemingly providing everyone with the opportunity to assume that title. Simultaneously, it has facilitated new avenues for some critics to reach their highest potential and enthrall audiences in exceptional ways, empowering them to embrace their digital vantage points. One thing is for certain: criticism can no longer afford to be ignorant of its politics and subjectivities in the way that it once could.

Today, music critics are neither publicists nor marketers nor gatekeepers. Critics are cartographers of culture, storytellers who must be committed to context. Although prone to many iterations of pressure across centuries, a critic's fundamental role will always be to guide an audience to new planes of understanding. And as long as this identity persists, the profession will remain relevant—and perhaps even vital—to the music ecosystem and society at large.

---

179 "Library," The Black Music History Library, accessed October 14, 2020.

AFTER LAUGHTER, AFTERMATH

Revisiting Music in Crisis

I am fleeing New York, revisiting Paramore's "Told You So" through ailing wired headphones on the tensest flight I've ever been on. I am curled up in a window seat that I have hurriedly disinfected, while a middle-aged woman flanks me to my left on the aisle, a personal Purell in hand. I suppose nobody has mustered up the courage to snag the middle seat, which serves as a free-floating forum for awkward glances and accidental elbows throughout our journey to Los Angeles. Sci-fi movies have always assured me that if the world ever goes to shit, we'll all start eating each other. Instead, we hold our breath behind surgical masks, surveilling our fellow subjects in silence. Hayley Williams whispers about being thrust into a fire into my ears against the hum of our aircraft cabin's white noise, no coughs brave enough to interrupt. I'm hungover.

My girlfriend, who flew back home a few days before me, picks me up from LAX with her father. It's pouring, an omen of dystopia for a city that's been defined by its seasonal immunity since long before I was born. As we small talk our way down the uncharacteristically barren 405 freeway, Trump declares the coronavirus pandemic a national emergency. Fuck—I left my eczema cream in our East Village apartment.

My sister opens the door for me when they drop me home; I no longer have a key. My dog, Lily, vies for my attention by climbing up my leg before getting bored by the time I set my oversized suitcase down, brimming with clothes for *who knows how long as soon as it's safe I guess but I think I mean I hope I'll be back soon I hope.* My sister's housemate, a close family friend, greets me in the kitchen with a state-sanctioned elbow tap.

"Strange how we find ourselves exactly where we left off," laments Hayley into my ears on another track, "Grudges."[180] I guess I'm home.

I WhatsApp my parents to let them know I've arrived. They are quarantined in India, having moved there after I left for college, renting the house to my sister as she completes a PhD program at UCLA until their imminent return. I'm grateful that they're alone and far away from us, since they're in their 60s, at high risk of suffering greatly if infected. Still, their absence is unsettling. They typically visit LA around the same times that I do, over Thanksgiving and weddings and New Year's and summer breaks. This time, I'm entering a different family unit than the one I grew up in, under very different circumstances.

---

180 Paramore, "Grudges," by Hayley Nicole Williams, Zach Farro, and Taylor Benjamin York, track 8, on *After Laughter* (Nashville: Fueled by Ramen), 2017.

My mom, a Mindfulness practitioner, radiates "Zen" over video chat. She is visibly relieved that my sister and I have finally started taking the virus seriously, sheltered in the same house, dedicated to taking precautions. Weeks ago, she called me in a frenzy, urging me to buy hand sanitizer for my apartment and to avoid concerts and subway poles, effective immediately. In a haze, I dismissed her cautions as maternal paranoia. I was too high—high off of the momentum of becoming the person I'd always wanted to be, three months from graduating from my dream school, on the brink of securing a sexy full-time job, of being irrationally stressed about studying for a take-home midterm for the last class I needed to meet my requirements and, not so secretly, loving it all. Now, all the details that have until recently driven my daily life seem silly at best, aimless at worst.

I haul my suitcase upstairs, barreling into my childhood bedroom. Its walls blind me, as they always do. A green so limey it's obnoxious, they are adorned with mementos from my high school years. I stare at the countless selfies of me and my bright-teethed friends at two o'clock in the morning sleepovers at Carlos' house, quirky moments at can't-miss-end-of-spring parties, tidbits of carefree joy during school assemblies, Teavana in hand. I stare at the cutout from my school newspaper's feature on senior prom night—my girlfriend and I wore Indian attire to the event, runner ups for prom king and queen, just months before we attended NYU together. In nearly every photo, my woefully unbearded face takes up at least 40 percent of the frame, since I was always the one who suggested we capture the moment. Nestled amongst these digital portraits are the curated accomplishments of my past: *AP Scholar with Distinction* (why?)*, Finalist in the*

Hollywood Songwriting Contest, my Early Decision acceptance letter from NYU. Accompanying them are the emblems of my obsessive streaks: a lopsided *Halo 3* poster, three hastily printed *Harry Potter and the Deathly Hallows* (Part 2!) postcards, an Amoeba Music sticker and Lady Gaga's "Applause" single cover (the one with the clown makeup, fittingly).

Highlight reels are funny things; they don't work super well when you're the one who captured the footage. I stare at this tapestry of memories that I once crafted so earnestly, and I bite my pinky nail down to its core. Pity—I feel pity. Pity for the boy who used to wake up so uncomfortable in his own skin that he relied on external indicators of his worth to energize him for yet another exhausting day of feeling—inadequate? Mediocre? Repressed? Who the hell is he? Didn't I get rid of him a while ago?

Others in my shoes might see a shimmery, insta-friendly adolescence. But I am struck by the film left behind, the cruel words from taunters I tried to redact, the lonely nights when I felt so out of place that I craved the chance to move coasts as soon as I could.

"I can feel that we've changed, and we're better this way," Hayley sings.[181] Here I am, coexisting with the ghost whose place I thought I'd taken for good, unexpectedly, indefinitely.

Weeks pass. Shit goes down. Over what would have been my spring break, I'm sick in bed with coronavirus, barely able to lift my upper body, but far more concerned about what's ensuing beyond my walls. Death tolls rise around the

---

181 Ibid.

country and the world. My friends are evicted from school, some without homes to return to. My aunt falls sick. Dua Lipa's album, presciently titled *Future Nostalgia,* comes and goes. It stops raining in LA. India, and my parents, go into lockdown. Lady Gaga postpones her album. The hikes close. I impulse buy noise-cancelling earbuds. The running trails stay open. My best friend turns twenty-two over Zoom. I try Wendy's drive-thru for the first time. My housemate files for unemployment. I develop an at-home espresso addiction.

Once recovered, I attempt to build a routine amidst the chaos. I start going for daily runs. I continue to blast Paramore's *After Laughter* as much as I can, newly able to decipher every individual howl and rhythmic production element in surround sound. Like Hayley, I am "Caught in the Middle," whooshing past my masked neighbors in the afternoon heat on the same loop I do every day, unable to either look back or look far ahead. This next chapter is precarious, for me, for all of us. But maybe there's a purpose in feeling nostalgic for the future that never came to be, for dwelling in the awkward empty seat between denial and acceptance. Maybe not.

Every sprint, half a mile longer by day, is fortified by the album that turned a routinely teased pop-punk band into profound mixologists of '80s synth-pop and soft rock upon its critically lauded release in 2017. I've loved Paramore as a source of musical pleasure and excitement since middle school, but these days, I *rely* on them. Their poetry affords me emotional clarity; desperate, I dwell on every word.

There are the albums we turn to for escapism, to dance away the pain, to sink into our fantasies. And then there are the albums that we turn to to illuminate the truth, in all its melancholic messiness. In the most unprecedented era of my life, and the lives of everyone around me, a piece of art that offers lucidity is just as appreciated as an elongated, warm, touchy-feely hug would be.

On "26," an acoustic lullaby, Hayley insists on the importance of holding onto hope as we grow older. I'll do my best.

In some ways, Paramore's evolution resembles my own. The band may have traded in poison-rich, roaring guitar riffs for beach-friendly basslines and hooky adlibs, but the emotional core of who they are has remained consistent. They might have gone from a joke some subcultures enjoyed to respected members of the broader musical canon, but their quirky theatricality has been fixed in place. Their lyrics are still existential, unabashed angst marinating in every measure. Their sonic scaffolding has become summery and bright instead of brutal and threatening. But its interior reveals the same old prison cell, newly decked in fairy lights, yet equally as constrained. It's this very dissonance that has started to help me understand my own situation.

I like the idea that you can grow and mature in dramatic and drastic and daring ways, but all the while stay the same at your center, demons and all. Maybe both can be true at once.

Usually, I'm intoxicated by the idea of constantly improving. I'm the king of scrutinizing former versions of myself, of admiring how much I've changed and discarding who I used to be, physically, socially, intellectually. The product of two metropoles, I have lived and sworn by the virtue of forward motion, the same fickle myth that lures the music industry into most of its messes, the myth that produced a global economy championed by leaders so obsessed with an insatiable growth model that they stretched finite resources so far until something big inevitably burst. That something happened to be the health apparatus, the most vital cornerstone of society, and the live music ecosystem was one of many casualties that followed. Who knows what's next?

On the cusp of my adult life, I am led to begin the process of rejecting this mythical linearity. My unfettered sense of pedestrian NYC invincibility has been challenged by the neighborly dynamics I now engage with regularly, once again. Is this a good thing? My hair is growing unruly, longer than it's been since my senior year of high school, and faded away has the fancy fade that my cheeks have become accustomed to on the East Coast. Am I still the "new me" I've gotten used to seeing in the mirror? I can only plan my schedule day by day, instead of micromanaging years in advance. Can I still be stable even if I'm not completely in control? I'm starting to think that these self-induced, internal tests might matter more than speeding through school exams. I'm starting to think that in this purgatory, I'm actually growing up.

People have been saying that the coronavirus crisis should put everything into context. It's the time for us to open up our hearts to forgiveness, to make connections with the people—and the records—who might have drifted away from us, for who knows how long we really have to make amends.

I've wasted years holding a grudge on the person I used to be. It's taken moving home early, losing all my pillars of normalcy, and cocooning myself into a contemplative album to realize that the two "selves" of my experience aren't as distinctive as I'd like to believe. Who I am now wouldn't exist without who I was then. Who I will become is an avatar of both. In ninth grade, back when Paramore's biggest hit was 2009's "The Only Exception," an anonymous user left me a note on my ask.fm page that cut deep: "ur weird, and you have dry ass lips." Rude, yes. But hey, at least one of those things is still true! New York has taught me to embrace who I am. Moving back has taught me that I must do the same with who I used to be.

On "Pool," *After Laughter's* magnum opus, Hayley belts about her resistance to giving up. It's Saturday, and I'm driving down the Pacific Coast Highway at eighty miles per hour, my girlfriend, also two weeks post-recovery, sitting in shotgun. As per advisories, we do not plan on leaving the car, masks and snacks and headphones resting on the backseat. The sun hovers as we hum along to the ice-cream-truck-chime countermelody that frames the track, booming out of my speakers. For miles, we cruise, fleeing nothing, going nowhere, relishing our grief. The waves look the same as they always have.

EPILOGUE

Listen to What You Love, Carry Your Own Umbrella

What if we were to accept the radical possibility that all music taste is subjective?

It's an idea that's been contentious for eons. In the later years of the eighteenth century, the rise of romanticism sparked contentious debates regarding the optimal role of music in European society and culture.[182] Composers such as Germany's E.T.A. Hoffmann and Richard Wagner embraced emerging artistic developments of the movement, while critics such as Austrian aesthetic theorist Eduard Hanslick subscribed to a far more conservative framework, resisting the individualistic tendencies of his opponents in favor of an examination of music that was far more formulaic. Whereas Hanslick maintained that the quality of a piece of music should be determined objectively, by virtue of its structural components, Hoffmann and Wagner believed in evaluating musical pieces subjectively, based

---

182 Anthony Burton, *A Performer's Guide to the Music of the Classical Period* (London: Associated Board of the Royal Schools of Music, 2002).

on our ability as listeners to interpret from them a sense of mystical vitality.[183]

Today, in Latin America, people regularly eat bugs, considered to be markers of high-class dining, a phenomenon which we neighbors up north find downright repulsive.[184] Up here, we glorify meals that center lobster, decadent and damaging to most any wallet. Yet lobsters are nocturnal bottom feeders, as verminous as insects, historically relegated to servants and pets.[185]

I posit that musical taste is similar to gustatory taste. How can we detach our perceptions of the value of pieces of music (or meat) without considering the culturally, socially, and individually perpetuated forces that have shaped our palettes since we first entered the world?

I, for one, enjoy music that makes me feel. I crave the motivational alternative anthem that energizes me when I am traversing the streets of New York City. I rely on the acoustic demo that provides catharsis when I am reflecting against the railings of the Hudson River. As soon as I hear the dramatic pair of hammer strokes that introduce Beethoven's "Eroica," I am filled with a sense of heroic optimism, thrilled by

---

183 Wayne Senner, *The Critical Reception of Beethoven's Compositions by his German Contemporaries* (Lincoln: University of Nebraska Press, 1999); Bryan Simmons, ed., *Richard Wagner's Prose Works,* Translated by William Ashton Ellis (London: Kegan Paul, 1894); Eduard Hanslick, *On the Musically Beautiful: A Contribution towards the Revision of the Aesthetics of Music* (New York: Da Capo, 1974).

184 Dana Goodyear, "Grub," *The New Yorker,* August 8, 2011.

185 Erica Schecter, "Lobster Used to Be 'The Cockroach of the Sea' and Only Fed to Servants and Cats," *Foodbeast,* February 13, 2014.

boundless suspense and tension; each line of the symphony seems to push a plot forward, a plot that I will never objectively be able to deconstruct, but whose significance I can certainly absorb on account of its experiential dynamism.

Does it stroke my ego when an album I love scores a *Pitchfork* 8+, a *Billboard* Hot 100 top-five single, or the Metacritic "universal acclaim" badge? Of course it does! As I've touched on throughout our journey, it is gratifying to be affirmed by the cultures you belong to, maybe even better to share ideas with fanatic subcultures that oppose the dominant culture. Everyone wants to belong to a community, whether conventional or contrarian.

Still, I'd like to think that the value I derive from the art I'm experiencing is meaningful on my own terms, and not the external myth of objectivity that actually represents other people's sonic spheres, or rather, *institutional* spheres—certainly not the unfettered truth, whatever that concept even means in the hyper-connected and hyper-polarized digital age.

If the internet disappeared tomorrow, I'm certain that Phoenix's "If I Ever Feel Better" would remain one of my favorite songs. It's not just because of its fade-in synthetic strings that conjure in it an air of sweet melancholy, or its bubble wrap-buoyant bassline, or its crying-on-the-dance-floor lyrical arch that can match almost any of my moods. It's also because that song reminds me of other songs in my listening repertoire—Toro y Moi's chillwave synths that got me through my sophomore year of college, Fall Out Boy's angsty poetry that was a staple of my sixteenth year, Paramore's rhythmic existentialism that I've adored since junior high (and, as I've divulged, depended on in recent times).

It's also because I listened to that song on repeat in a depressive state during the first summer after college started, when my response to loved ones who reached out to help me was to send them the most crucial chorus of the song (timestamp 1:03). I promise I'll get back to you, "If I Ever Feel Better," I'd say.

I wonder if my sentimental attachment to the song is simply inextricable from my analytical perspective. I'm sure, if I tried hard and flexed some business-savvy muscles, I could place my head in the mind of an "average listener" and think about it "objectively." I could sterilize the emotion out of my connection to it and evaluate it like a shampoo or a silk tie. But why try? I love it, and that love is mine.

True freedom is self-possession paired with impassioned possession of all that we hold dear. There's a time and a place for listening to others, and the rest of the time we should listen to and wholly possess whatever the (mic-drop) we want.

One of the beauties in believing in your own beat is that you don't have to silence anyone else to keep the melodies flowing. As we have explored, I don't believe it is a music executive or a music critic or a music streaming service's job to tell you how you feel about something. Let's let the algorithms aggregate. Let's let the marketers market. Let's let the critics critique. It's useful, even illuminating to hear respected voices make their claims. But don't forget that you, too, are a personal editor for the magazine in your mind, your own sonic compass. If Anthony Fantano, the self-proclaimed "busiest music nerd" on the internet were to quit YouTube tomorrow and never make another viral *Needle Drop* review, wouldn't you still want to know which album to dive into next?[186]

According to a *Music Business Worldwide* report, more than 1.2 million tracks get added to Spotify every month.[187] Every week, music companies are invented, disbanded, merged, and acquired. Every day, millions of songs are consumed by millions of people, milliseconds apart, across the globe. The soundstorm's gonna get even crazier, and you might as well carry your own umbrella.

Many music listening expeditions are seldom appreciated by gatekeepers, from jazz to Jepsen, from classical to K-pop. Underdog albums often generate cult followings against the context of commercial disaster. Experimental projects often take years to find their rightful audience. Seemingly robotic video game scores often serve as pivotal sources of childhood comfort for their legions of players.

For one, *The Sims 2* build-buy mode soundtrack likely doesn't tickle the fancies of many musicologists, but it plunges me back into hours spent creating digital families on my ailing PC desktop, sipping on the frothy banana milkshakes my mom loved to treat me to after long days at elementary school, its harpsichord synth etched into my eardrums.

"It's the Time to Disco," a Bollywood banger from the 2003 movie *Kal Ho Naa Ho,* might be dismissed by most around

---

186 Sean Burch, "How Anthony Fantano Became 'The Internet's Busiest Music Nerd' on YouTube," *The Wrap,* October 9, 2019.

187 Tim Ingham, "Nearly 40,000 Tracks Are Now Being Added to Spotify Every Single Day," *Music Business Worldwide,* April 29, 2019.

the world as a fun, albeit tepid pop song, but to me, it ushers in flashbacks of my most joyous nights of college, dancing and singing at rowdy pregames with like-minded friends who would soon become my lifelong confidants.

When you tell someone that a song they like "isn't good, *objectively*," you're ignoring the fact that you are in no position to understand how they are perceiving it. For you, it might be noise. For them, it could be life-affirming.

How about this? You keep your umbrella, and I'll keep mine. Let's swap every now and then! Maybe you'll find something you love. Maybe I will too. Even if a track's not for me, I promise I'll appreciate that it means something to you. You are your own subject; let's let everyone else be theirs too.

At three o'clock last night, with the aid of a drink (or three), I wrote a song of my own that reflects the characteristics I love most in the music I listen to. I enjoy a wide variety of genres, but now that I'm in my early twenties, I've narrowed down a type of song that I am particularly drawn to at this snapshot of time. This type of song melds multiple genres, typically taking the shape of an indie-leaning track with pop structure, R&B influence, and a mix of generous synth usage and organic instruments. These songs come from artists across the sonic spectrum, but they share structural elements. They all lead me to contemplate, to dance, and above all, to wish I had written them myself.

Although I didn't realize it when the melodies and verses popped into my head after being inspired by the catchphrase on a neon green greeting card my friend Kai sent me for my (virtual) college graduation (it said "did it just get hotter in here?"), this song ended up reflecting many of the notions I seek out as a music listener.

Subconsciously, I wrote this song as a message to myself, a seamless addition to the proverbial playlist that is my life path. I'm in quarantine, kind of employed but kind of jobless at the same time, writing this book and thrilled about it, but admittedly terrified about what's to come and what I'm going to make of my life—(if you're reading this right now, please know that freshly post-grad Saransh truly appreciates it so much).

A quiet but potent voice in my head is telling me to just chill out. The song I wrote, consequently, is about being on the cusp of real adulthood and feeling at once a poisonous sense of self-doubt but also knowing I need to harness my childlike spirit to thrive in my next phase.

This new chapter could, if I allow it, be a reformation of my youth and a newfound opportunity to be a child, fearless, sponge-like, and willing to let the environments that fill me with warmth heal me. For me, that environment is New York City, and I'm finally moving back next week to mark the start of the summer…and the rest of my life. Maybe, once back in this fast-paced, sweat-stained, hand-picked home of mine, I'll turn the demo I made into a daily mindset.

> "Polluted clouds produce polluted minds
> as the dusk dissolves into the night
> I see my youth reflected in the skies
> My infancy returns through city lights"

Writing a song is exhilarating, a portal to the visceral high of crafting something from scratch. Promoting music is super exciting in its own way, an opportunity to help art reach its rightful audience. Critiquing music is stimulating too, a way to clarify, consider, and connect with the context that surrounds the sound. But it all comes back to listening. For those who pray to music, listening is at the very core of what it means to be alive. I know for a fact that I'm not alone in feeling this way.

> "Be who you are
> Do what you love
> It's your world for now"

Many say that we are born with perfect senses of self; we enter this world at the centers of our own universes. As we grow up, society wedges a rift between each of us and our individualized confidence with every billboard, *Billboard*™ chart, tabloid, and rule book that tells us that who we are and how we think without the outside noise they impose on us isn't good enough. But one of the most liberating realizations that any of us can experience is that we can render ourselves immune with the exercise of a mental filter, the wielding of a musical umbrella.

> "Be who you are
> Be a child"

I wonder if the future of music is an ecosystem that encourages us to cherish those umbrellas. I wonder if the future of music is a re-emphasis on local economies, digital infrastructures that are segmented by markets and communities, and critical perspectives grounded in subjectivity. I wonder if innovation arises out of the very stuff that makes us different, not what resigns us to conformity and archaic systems that might be limiting us from our fullest potential.

I believe music itself is beautiful because it is evocative in this individualized way. How wonderful would it be if the ecosystem that envelopes it magnified that ethos on a structural level?

I wonder if, for three and a half minutes, you can be the center of your own universe at the same time as everyone else is the center of theirs, respective earbuds in respective ears, respecting one another.

Here's some music that I've loved recently. Perhaps, you'll love it too. Either way, we'll both be just fine.

- "After the Storm" by Kali Uchis, Tyler, the Creator, and Bootsy Collins
- "Only If" by Steve Lacy
- "Reflection of the Moon" by BE GOOD
- "Strangemirror" by Shyamala
- "Cranes in the Sky" by Solange
- "Power On" by James Blake
- "Bedroom" by Litany
- "Lost in Yesterday" by Tame Impala
- "You Seemed so Happy" by The Japanese House
- "Sober" by Lorde
- "Why We Ever" by Hayley Williams
- "Chemical" by Beck
- "Runner" by Tennis

- "Closetowhy" by Parcels
- "Touch" by Shura
- "Blinding My Vision" by K. Roosevelt
- "No Going Back" by Yuno
- "Campus" by Vampire Weekend
- "Pantyhose" by TV Girl
- "Can I" by Sanjana
- "Laughing with a Mouth of Blood" by St. Vincent
- "La pluie" by Orelsan and Stromae
- "Lucky I Got What I Want" by Jungle
- "Girl Like You" by Toro y Moi
- "Born to Bleed" by Red Hearse
- "Play" by iamamiwhoami
- "Flowers & Superpowers" by Wafia
- "Pink + White" by Frank Ocean
- "Unputdownable" by Róisín Murphy
- "If I Ever Feel Better" by Phoenix

Now, tell me—what have you been listening to?

ACKNOWLEDGMENTS

When I was seven years old, I wrote my first "book," the tale of a teddy bear who overcame being stranded in the desert by fostering friendships with locals in a nearby village. Fifteen years later, I've learned that publishing a real book, too, takes the warmth, the support, and the spirit of community that only a village could provide. Thank you for being a cornerstone of that village—I am so grateful for your role in making one of my childhood dreams a reality.

First and foremost, I'd like to thank my parents, Bhagwan Chowdhry and Swati Desai, for always championing me to be whomever I want to be.

Thank you to my girlfriend and best friend, Abby Shaum, for keeping me sane and for motivational hugs aplenty.

Thank you to New Degree Press and the Creator Institute—namely Eric Koester, Cass Lauer, Stephanie McKibben, Brian Bies, Gjorgji Pejkovski, Stojan Velichkov, Zoran Maksimovic, and Nick Mancuso—for encouraging me and guiding me throughout this process.

Thank you to my writing teachers, whose stories have inspired me to share my own: Ms. Staake, Ms. Kern, Mr. Michaelson, Mr. Weber, Professor Amanda Petrusich, Professor Ben Ratliff, Professor Lizzie Valverde, Professor Elizabeth Molkou, Professor Jeffrey Eugenides—I am so lucky to have benefited from your wisdom.

Thank you to my musical mentors, who have fueled my passion for the power of sound: Sanjukta Dasgupta, Rodger Guerrero, Kwami Coleman, Lee Dannay, and Marcie Allen.

Thank you to NYU's Gallatin School of Individualized Study, my alma mater, for believing in me and supporting this project with a grant and an exploratory education that I will forever cherish.

Thank you to each of the brilliant humans who took time out of their busy days to muse with me: Kristen Arnold, Blu DeTiger, Nick DeMasi, Noah Kaplan, Rosie Kaplan, Krishna Gaur, Francesca Walker, Wooseok Ki, Jon Links, Jason Lipshutz, Amanda Petrusich, and Jenzia Burgos.

Thank you to everyone who pre-ordered the book, helped spread the word to garner momentum, offered insights on my drafts, and allowed me to craft and share a body of work that I am proud of. During the madness that is this *Soundstorm*, I appreciate you lending me your umbrellas!

Aaron Raus	Amanda Hembree
Abby Luo	Amy Dong
Adam Yaron	Anaïs Kessler
Alice Su Jin Nam	Annik Irving

Anushka Lakhani
Aoife Kingsbury
Avery Bonner
Bebe Howell
Bharatan Kandaswamy
Caitlyn Lubas
Carlos Guanche
Chandra Kelley
Chloë Combes
Dylan Schifrin
Elias Rosas
Eric Chen
Fauzia Farooqui
Gabriela Naumnik
Gigi Martinez
Giulia Delle Femine
Hannah Benson
Hunter Wolff
Isik Surdum
Jeeyoon Lim
Jon Merkin
Julia Mates
Juliet Park
Kahaia Voelkl

Kai Byron
Kashyap Kompella
Katerina Jennings
Katie Collins
Katie Sing
Kelly Morrison
Kevin Weiskirch
Kylie McManus
Larry Guindine
Lauren Chiriboga
Lindsey Alpaugh
Louisa Brady
Maddy Kahn
Madhu Vishwanathan
Mallika Velamuri
Marie Nercessian
Maura Leichliter
Max Schorr
Mehaa Desai
Mihir Phatak
Mike Leichliter
Milan Meena
Nancy Shankman
Nathalie Rebolledo

Noah Broxmeyer
Paheli Desai-Chowdhry
Pamela Jew
Pravina Cooper
Rachel Porter
Rahul Ranade
Ramana Sonti
Ravi Durairaj
Ryan Finley
Sanjana Deshmukh
Sanji Nerkar
Savannah Guy
Scott Durbin
Shashii Asnani

Shelley Jain
Sonia Das
Sumit Agarwal
Talia Resnick
Tanaya Deshmukh
Vaiju Valsangkar
Vaishali Deshmukh
Valerie Stepanova
Vincent Duque
Yeonhee Yang
Yif Chen
Zahir Byam
Zoe Searles

...*thank you!*

APPENDIX

INTRODUCTION: WEATHERING THE SOUNDSTORM, TOGETHER
Dredge, Stuart. "Goldman Sachs: 'Global Music Revenue Will Drop by 25% in 2020'." *Music Ally*, May 18, 2020.
https://musically.com/2020/05/18/goldman-sachs-global-music-revenue-will-drop-by-25-in-2020/.

Lee, Wendy. "Creative Artists Agency Cuts, Furloughs Nearly 20% of Its Staff Amid Pandemic." *Los Angeles Times*, July 28, 2020.
https://www.latimes.com/entertainment-arts/business/story/2020-07-28/creative-artists-agency-cuts-furloughs-nearly-20-of-its-staff-amid-pandemic.

Sanchez, Daniel. "Goldman Sachs Says Global Music Revenues Will Reach $131 Billion by 2030." *Digital Music News*, June 5, 2019.
https://www.digitalmusicnews.com/2019/06/05/goldman-sachs-global-music-revenue/.

MUSIC'S MYTHIC NIGHT: DREAMS AND DISILLUSIONMENT AT THE GRAMMYS
Ahlgrim, Callie. "Tyler, the Creator Responded to Someone on Twitter Who Told Him He'd Never Win a Grammy 9 Years Ago." *Insider*, January 27, 2020.
https://www.insider.com/tyler-the-creator-grammy-win-tweet-reply-9-years-ago-2020-.

American Marketing Association Toronto. "Gen Zers Are Redefining Brand Loyalty." Blog. Updated December 14, 2017.
https://www.ama-toronto.com/blog/gen-zers-are-redefining-brand-loyalty.

Aswad, Jem. "Recording Academy Chief Harvey Mason Jr. on Social Change and What the 2021 Grammys Might Look Like." *Variety*, June 10, 2020.
https://variety.com/2020/music/news/grammy-awards-recording-academy-harvey-mason-1234630208/.

Berman, Judy. "Award Shows Are Dying. Is That Such a Bad Thing?" *TIME*, January 16, 2020.
https://time.com/5766190/award-shows-2020-relevance-essay/.

Blais-Billie, Braudie and Jazz Monroe. "SZA on Ctrl: "I Didn't Even Fuck with My Own Album."" *Pitchfork,* February 28, 2018. https://pitchfork.com/news/sza-on-ctrl-i-didnt-even-fuck-with-my-own-album/.

Butler, Bethonie. "The Recording Academy Is Imploding the Week before the Grammys. Here's What We Know." *The Washington Post,* January 23, 2020. https://www.washingtonpost.com/arts-entertainment/2020/01/22/recording-academy-is-imploding-week-before-grammys-heres-what-we-know/.

Cherie Hu (@CherieHu42). "This seems......... not better." Twitter, June 10, 2020. https://twitter.com/cheriehu42/status/1270750217390956544.

Flanagan, Andrew. "Grammy President Neil Portnow to Step Down in 2019." *NPR,* June 1, 2018. https://www.npr.org/sections/therecord/2018/06/01/615889769/grammy-president-neil-portnow-to-step-down-in-2019.

Giorgis, Hannah. "Parasite Won So Much More Than the Best Picture Oscar." *The Atlantic,* February 10, 2020. https://www.theatlantic.com/culture/archive/2020/02/parasite-oscars/606310/.

Koblin, John. "Grammy Awards Hit 12-Year Low in TV Viewers." *The New York Times,* January 27, 2020. https://www.nytimes.com/2020/01/27/business/media/grammy-awards-ratings.html.

Moore, Sam. "Justin Bieber to Miss 2018 Grammys Ceremony despite Being Nominated." *NME,* January 26, 2018. https://www.nme.com/news/music/justin-bieber-2018-grammys-snub-despite-being-nominated-2229236.

Nielsen. "The Grammy Effect: Sales and On-Demand Streams of Music Performed at the 60th Grammy Awards Surge." Insights. Updated February 5, 2018. https://www.nielsen.com/us/en/insights/article/2018/the-grammy-effect-sales-and-on-demand-streams-of-music-performed-surge/.

Rae, Bianca. "Variety Senior Music Editor Discusses Future of the Grammys." *Spectrum News 1,* January 25, 2020. https://spectrumnews1.com/ca/la-west/entertainment/2020/01/24/variety-senior-music-editor-discusses-future-of-the-grammys.

Sang, Zach. "Ariana Grande 'thank u, next' Interview." Zach Sang Show. Uploaded on February 9, 2019. YouTube video, 1:23:26. https://youtu.be/fpl8v3jiuNU.

Stutz, Colin. "Drake Won't Be at the Grammy Awards." *Billboard,* January 30, 2017. https://www.billboard.com/articles/news/grammys/7670151/drake-missing-grammys-justin-bieber-kanye-west.

Stutz, Colin. "Frank Ocean Explains His Decision to Sit Out 2017 Grammys." *Billboard,* November 15, 2016. https://www.billboard.com/articles/columns/hip-hop/7580396/frank-ocean-explains-sitting-out-2017-grammys.

Willman, Chris. "Dr. Luke: The Billboard Cover Story." *Billboard,* September 3, 2010. https://www.billboard.com/articles/news/956518/dr-luke-the-billboard-cover-story.

Yandoli, Krystie Lee. "Here's the Drama Between Ariana Grande and the Grammys." *Buzzfeed,* February 6, 2019. https://www.buzzfeednews.com/article/krystieyandoli/ariana-grande-grammys.

Yoo, Noah. "Grammys 2019: Ariana Grande Wins First Grammy." *Pitchfork,* February 10, 2019. https://pitchfork.com/news/grammys-2019-ariana-grande-wins-best-pop-vocal-album/.

IDEALISTIC INELASTICITY: BURSTING THE TICKETING BUBBLE

Alternative Press Magazine. "Halsey Announces Intimate Era Shows, Fans Speculate Next Single." *Alternative Press Magazine,* May 2, 2019. https://www.altpress.com/news/halsey-webster-hall-shows-badlands-hfk/.

Aswad, Jem. "Senators Klobuchar, Blumenthal, Booker Push Justice Department for Competitive Concert Ticket Prices." *Variety,* May 14, 2020. https://variety.com/2020/biz/news/klobuchar-blumenthal-booker-ticket-pricing-live-nation-1234607061/.

Brooks, Dave. "Live Nation Planning to Pause Arena Tours Due to Coronavirus." *Billboard,* March 12, 2020. https://www.billboard.com/articles/business/touring/9333748/live-nation-global-pause-tours-concerts-coronavirus.

Chesler, Josh. "Rage Against the Machine Raises $3 Million Combating Ticket Scalpers." *Spin,* February 16, 2020. https://www.spin.com/2020/02/rage-against-machine-ticket-scalpers-charity/#:~:text=Rage%20Against%20the%20Machine's%20 plan,as%2Doverpriced%20official%20charity%20tickets.

Gensler, Andy. "2019 Business Analysis." *Pollstar,* December 16, 2019. https://www.pollstar.com/Chart/2019/12/BusinessAnalysis_792.pdf.

Knopper, Steve. "How Kanye West Made His Saint Pablo Stage Fly." *Rolling Stone,* September 7, 2016. https://www.rollingstone.com/music/music-features/how-kanye-west-made-his-saint-pablo-stage-fly-101150/.

Mitchell, John. "Lady Gaga's 'Born This Way Ball' Stage Biggest Ever Built to Tour." *MTV,* May 2, 2012. http://www.mtv.com/news/2582266/lady-gagas-born-this-way-ball-stage-biggest-ever-built-to-tour/.

Peoples, Glenn. "Live Nation Revenue Down 98% Due to Pandemic Shut Downs." *Billboard,* August 5, 2020. https://www.billboard.com/index.php/articles/business/touring/9429902/live-nation-q2-2020-earnings-revenue-concerts-coronavirus.

Schneiderman, Eric T. *Obstructed View: What's Blocking New Yorkers from Getting Tickets.* New York: Attorney General's Office, 2016.

Shaw, Lucas. "Concerts Are More Expensive Than Ever, and Fans Keep Paying Up." *Bloomberg*, September 10, 2019.
https://www.bloomberg.com/news/articles/2019-09-10/concerts-are-more-expensive-than-ever-and-fans-keep-paying-up.

Weiner, Zoe. "Taylor Swift's Snake—Whose Name Is Karyn, BTW—Stole the Show at the 2018 American Music Awards." *Glamour*, October 10, 2018.
https://www.glamour.com/story/taylor-swift-snake-american-music-awards.

DON'T CALL BLU DETIGER AN OVERNIGHT SUCCESS: DISCIPLINE AND DETOURS IN THE DIGITAL AGE

Ingham, Tim. "'For a Lot of These TikTok Hits, the Artists Could Be an Avatar—It Wouldn't Matter'." *Music Business Worldwide*, July 21, 2020.
https://www.musicbusinessworldwide.com/vydia-roy-lamanna-this-new-generation-of-managers-dont-know-the-rules-and-therefore-dont-abide-by-the-rules/.

Leight, Elias. "Surprising No One, TikTok Is Driving a Lot of New-Artist Growth." *Rolling Stone*, February 28, 2020.
https://www.rollingstone.com/pro/news/chartmetric-breakthrough-artists-report-958401/.

Leskin, Paige. "TikTok Surpasses 2 Billion Downloads and Sets a Record for App Installs in a Single Quarter." *Business Insider*, April 30, 2020.
https://www.businessinsider.com/tiktok-app-2-billion-downloads-record-setting-q1-sensor-tower-2020-4.

Romero, Luis E. "Overnight Success Is a Myth—Here Is Why." *Forbes*, August 8, 2016.
https://www.forbes.com/sites/luisromero/2016/08/08/overnight-success-is-bs-here-is-why/#642945d25e2c.

Stassen, Murray. "The Hottest Independent Artists in the World: Blu DeTiger, Calynn Green, Dirty Blond, Olive Amun & Sara Kays." *Music Business Worldwide*, May 29, 2020.
https://www.musicbusinessworldwide.com/the-hottest-independent-artists-in-the-world-blue-detiger-calynn-green-dirty-blond-olive-amun-sara-kays/.

Tolentino, Jia. *Trick Mirror: Reflections on Self-Delusion*. New York: Random House, 2019.

THE SPOTIFY DILEMMA: MUSIC'S MESSIEST DIVORCE

Bandcamp Help Center. "What Pricing Performs Best?" Selling FAQ. Accessed October 14, 2020.
https://get.bandcamp.help/hc/en-us/articles/360007802534-What-pricing-performs-best-.

Desai-Chowdhry, Saransh. "In Defense of Music Streaming: How Spotify Helped Me Grieve When I Didn't Think I Deserved To." *The Tab NYU*, April 6, 2018.
https://thetab.com/us/nyu/2018/04/06/in-defense-of-music-streaming-how-spotify-helped-me-grieve-when-i-didnt-think-i-deserved-to-11572.

Dredge, Stuart. "Bandcamp's Monthly Sales Are up by 122% Year-on-Year." *Music Ally*, September 23, 2020.
https://musically.com/2020/09/23/bandcamps-monthly-sales-are-up-by-122-year-on-year/.

Hogan, Mark. "The Record Industry Expects a Windfall. Where Will the Money Go?" *Pitchfork,* May 30, 2019.
https://pitchfork.com/features/article/the-record-industry-expects-a-windfall-where-will-the-money-go/.

Ingham, Tim. "Should Spotify Change the Way It Pays Artists?" *Rolling Stone,* December 7, 2018.
https://www.rollingstone.com/music/music-features/should-spotify-change-the-way-it-pays-artists-763986/.

Liz Pelly. "About." Accessed October 14, 2020.
https://lizpelly.com/about.

Music Business Worldwide. "Thom Yorke Slams Spotify as Albums Are Removed." *Music Business Worldwide,* July 14, 2013.
https://www.musicbusinessworldwide.com/thom-yorke-slams-spotify-albums-removed/.

Pelly, Liz. "The Problem with Muzak." *The Baffler,* December 1, 2017.
https://thebaffler.com/salvos/the-problem-with-muzak-pelly.

Roberts, Randall. "Q&A: Joanna Newsom Calls Spotify 'a Villainous Cabal' and 'a Garbage System'." *Los Angeles Times,* October 18, 2015.
https://www.latimes.com/entertainment/music/posts/la-et-ms-joanna-newsom-spotify-villainous-cabal-garbage-system-20151015-story.html.

Spotify. "Audio-First." Newsroom. Updated February 6, 2019.
https://newsroom.spotify.com/2019-02-06/audio-first/.

Spotify. "Celebrating a Decade of Discovery on Spotify." Newsroom. Updated October 10, 2018.
https://newsroom.spotify.com/2018-10-10/celebrating-a-decade-of-discovery-on-spotify/.

Spotify. "We're Closing the Upload Beta Program. Here's What Artists Need to Know." Artists. Updated July 1, 2019.
https://artists.spotify.com/blog/we%27re-closing-the-upload-beta-program.

Statista. "Spotify's Premium Subscribers 2015–2020." Music. Updated August 21, 2010.
https://www.statista.com/statistics/244995/number-of-paying-spotify-subscribers/.

Swift, Taylor. "For Taylor Swift, the Future of Music Is a Love Story." *The Wall Street Journal,* July 7, 2014.
https://online.wsj.com/articles/for-taylor-swift-the-future-of-music-is-a-love-story-1404763219.

Wikiwand. "Criticism of Spotify." Wikipedia. Accessed October 14, 2020.
https://www.wikiwand.com/en/Criticism_of_Spotify.

MOURNING MY RECORD STORES: THE LINEAGE OF THE LOCAL MUSIC ECONOMY

Atkinson, Will. "Record Shops Sell a Hands-on Experience. Now They're Adapting to a Hands-off World." *INDY Week,* July 8, 2020.
https://indyweek.com/music/features/local-record-shops-coronavirus/.

Dinges, Gary. "Record Stores Were Already Struggling before the Pandemic. Here's How They're Staying Afloat Now." *USA Today,* June 12, 2020. https://www.usatoday.com/story/entertainment/music/2020/06/12/coronavirus-independent-record-stores-struggling-shutdowns-persist/3157326001/.

Kelley, Caitlyn. "The Raconteurs' 'Help Us Stranger' Becomes Their First No. 1 Album on the Billboard 200." *Forbes,* June 30, 2019. https://www.forbes.com/sites/caitlinkelley/2019/06/30/the-raconteurs-help-us-stranger-becomes-their-first-no-1-album-on-the-billboard-200/#d374f21acd59.

Leight, Elias. "Vinyl Is Poised to Outsell CDs for the First Time since 1986." *Rolling Stone,* September 6, 2019. https://www.rollingstone.com/pro/news/vinyl-cds-revenue-growth-riaa-880959/.

McKibben, Bill. *Deep Economy.* New York: St. Martin's Press, 2007.

Smith, Dylan. "More Indie Record Stores Are Calling It Quits—Steady Sounds, Dead Media Latest." *Digital Music News,* May 25, 2020. https://www.digitalmusicnews.com/2020/05/25/indie-record-stores-shutting-down/.

PRESERVING MAGIC, PROTECTING LIVELIHOODS: BEYOND NEW ORLEANS' MUSICAL ESCAPES

Aggour, Sarah. "New Orleans: The Culture of Resilient Music Arises after Katrina." *PCD Network,* April 10, 2017. https://pcdn.global/stories-of-impact/new-orleans-the-culture-of-resilient-music-arises-after-katrina/.

Brasted, Chelsea. "There Are Gaps in New Orleans' Music Industry. Business Leaders Hope to Fill Them." *NOLA.com,* January 25, 2019. https://www.nola.com/entertainment_life/music/article_59d99aec-1b7f-5d8f-b436-ff5fb655b68a.html.

Montgomery, David. "In a Self-Isolated World, New Orleans Musicians Fight to Beat Back the Silence." *The Washington Post,* April 9, 2020. https://www.washingtonpost.com/national/coronavirus-new-orleans-musicians/2020/04/09/fd5e2f84-774b-11ea-a130-df573469f094_story.html.

Mooney, Chris. "Loss of Louisiana Marshes That Protect New Orleans Is 'Probably Inevitable,' Study Finds." *The Washington Post,* May 22, 2020. https://www.washingtonpost.com/climate-environment/2020/05/22/new-orleans-wetlands-climatechange/.

New Orleans Musicians' Clinic. "About Us." Accessed October 14, 2020. https://neworleansmusiciansclinic.org/about-us/.

Preservation Hall. "Our Story." About. Accessed October 14, 2020. https://www.preservationhall.com/about/.

Raeburn, Bruce Boyd. "'They're Tryin' to Wash Us Away': New Orleans Musicians Surviving Katrina." *Journal of American History,* 94 (Dec. 2007): 812–819. http://archive.oah.org/special-issues/katrina/Raeburn5ceo.html?link_id=whi_jazzfuneral.

Ramsey, Jan. "By the Numbers: Sweet Home New Orleans Releases 2012 State of the New Orleans Music Community Report." *OffBeat Magazine,* May 1, 2013. https://www.offbeat.com/news/sweet-home-new-orleans-releases-2012-state-new-orleans-music-community-report/.

Sound Diplomacy. "New Orleans Music Economy Initiative (NOME)." New Orleans. Accessed October 14, 2020. https://www.sounddiplomacy.com/new-orleans#:~:text=The%20vision%20for%20the%20New,(music%20copyright)%20value%20stream.

World Population Review. "New Orleans, Louisiana Population 2020." US Cities. Accessed October 14, 2020. https://worldpopulationreview.com/us-cities/new-orleans-la-population.

FALSE INHERITANCE: THE OVERSATURATION OF THE SELF-TITLED ALBUM

Donnelly, Matthew Scott. "Paramore Bassist Quits, One Original Member Remains." *Pop Crush,* December 15, 2015. https://popcrush.com/paramore-bassist-jeremy-davis-quit/.

Fitzsimmons, Casey. "The Most Jaw-Dropping Moments from Demi Lovato's Documentary." *Soundigest,* October 24, 2017. https://soundigest.com/2017/10/24/4-jaw-dropping-moments-from-demi-lovatos-documentary/.

Lomax, Yasmine. "What's the Deal with Self-Titled Albums?" *Yasmine Lorax* (blog), August 11, 2019. https://yazminelomax.com/2019/08/11/whats-the-deal-with-self-titled-albums/.

The Editors of Encyclopaedia Britannica. "Tin Pan Alley." *Encyclopædia Britannica,* February 27, 2020. https://www.britannica.com/art/Tin-Pan-Alley-musical-history.

BOLLYWOOD, CALIFORNIA: NAVIGATING CULTURAL APPROPRIATION AS AN ABCD

Azalea, Iggy. "Iggy Azalea - Bounce (Official Music Video)." Iggy Azalea. Uploaded on May 5, 2013. YouTube video, 3:16. https://youtu.be/cI1A405jBqg.

Coldplay. "Coldplay - Hymn for the Weekend (Official Video)." Coldplay. Uploaded on January 29, 2016. YouTube video, 4:20. https://www.youtube.com/watch?v=YykjpeuMNEk.

Guha, Rohin. "Iggy Azalea Bounces Backwards with Disappointing Clichés." *The Aerogram,* May 28, 2013. https://theaerogram.com/iggy-azalea-bounces-backwards-with-disappointing-cliches/.

Hu, Cherie. "How India, The Global Music Industry's Sleeping Giant, Is Finally Waking Up." *Forbes,* September 23, 2017. https://www.forbes.com/sites/cheriehu/2017/09/23/how-india-the-global-music-industrys-sleeping-giant-is-finally-waking-up/#1387b74930bf.

Kaufman, Donna. "Should Selena Gomez Apologize for Wearing a Bindi at the MTV Movie Awards?" *Today*, April 17, 2013. https://www.today.com/popculture/selena-gomez-causes-controversy-wearing-bindi-mtv-movie-awards-I533548.

Lakshmin, Deepa. "I Was in India When Coldplay and Beyoncé's Video Dropped -- and I Don't See Cultural Appropriation." *MTV News*, February 4, 2016. http://www.mtv.com/news/2734844/coldplay-beyonce-hymn-weekend-cultural-appropriation-india/.

Prashad, Vijay. *The Karma of Brown Folk*. Minneapolis: U of Minnesota, 2000.

Rivera, Zayda. "Selena Gomez Urged to Apologize for Wearing Hindu Religious Ornament during MTV Performance." *NY Daily News*, April 16, 2013. https://www.nydailynews.com/entertainment/music-arts/selena-gomez-apologize-wearing-bindi-hindu-leaders-article-1.1318593.

Seacrest, Ryan. "Selena Gomez Premieres 'Come & Get It' PART 1 | Interview | On Air with Ryan Seacrest." On Air with Ryan Seacrest. Uploaded on April 8, 2013. YouTube video, 4:55.
https://youtu.be/d2diOotrpTA.

Sieczkowski, Cavan. "Selena Gomez Bindi: Hindu Leaders Demand Apology for MTV Movie Awards Costume." *HuffPost*, April 16, 2013. https://www.huffpost.com/entry/selena-gomez-bindi-mtv-movie-awards_n_3092129.

Vikaas, Kishwer. "ABCD: Who Are You Calling Confused?" *Asian American Writers' Workshop*, July 24, 2014.
https://aaww.org/abcd-a-short-history/.

WhoSampled. "Selena Gomez - Come & Get It." Accessed October 14, 2020. https://www.whosampled.com/sample/576577/Selena-Gomez-Come-%26-Get-It-Bollywood-Sounds-Dachee.

Young, James O. *Cultural Appropriation and the Arts*. Malden: Blackwell Publishing, 2009.

WHY BLAME BILLIE EILISH?: CONFRONTING THE CONVENTION OF INDUSTRY PLANTING

Arnold, Denis and Nigel Fortune. *The Monteverdi Companion*. New York: W.W. Norton & Company, 1968.

Bain, Katie. "A Day in the Life of Billie Eilish." *LNWY*, October 5, 2017. https://lnwy.co/read/introducing-billie-eilish/.

Charity, Justin. "What Is an Industry Plant?" *Complex*, October 20, 2016. https://www.complex.com/music/2015/06/what-is-an-industry-plant.

Coscarelli, Joe. "Billie Eilish Is Not Your Typical 17-Year-Old Pop Star. Get Used to Her." *The New York Times*, March 28, 2019.
https://www.nytimes.com/2019/03/28/arts/music/billie-eilish-debut-album.html.

Coscarelli, Joe. "Watch Billie Eilish and Her Family Talk about How They Make Music | Diary of a Song." *The New York Times.* Uploaded on April 1, 2019. YouTube video, 8:02. https://youtu.be/xeGT5uu_lRo.

Ghdust2. "Let's Talk: Billie Eilish." *Reddit.* https://www.reddit.com/r/LetsTalkMusic/comments/aiusyz/lets_talk_billie_eilish/.

Grein, Paul. "Grammys 2020: Billie Eilish Becomes the First Woman to Sweep the Big Four Grammys in One Night." *Billboard,* January 27, 2020. https://www.billboard.com/articles/news/awards/8549290/grammys-2020-billie-eilish-big-four-sweep.

Hamilton, Edith and Huntington Cairns. *The Collected Dialogues of Plato.* Princeton: Princeton University Press, 1989.

Ingham, Tim. "'Once You Help an Artist Build a Robust Business, a Lot Starts to Happen for Them'." *Music Business Worldwide,* March 31, 2020. https://www.musicbusinessworldwide.com/denzyl-feigelson-once-you-help-an-artist-build-a-robust-business-a-lot-starts-to-happen-for-them/.

LovingYouNowJake. "Billie Eilish Is overrated and kind of annoying." *Reddit.* https://www.reddit.com/r/unpopularopinion/comments/8mmhon/billie_eilish_is_overrated_and_kind_of_annoying/.

M.H. "Is Billie Eilish Really Changing Pop Stardom?" *The Economist,* April 5, 2019. https://www.economist.com/prospero/2019/04/05/is-billie-eilish-really-changing-pop-stardom?fsrc=scn%2Ftw%2Fte%2Fbl%2Fed%2Fauto.

Nattress, Katrina. "Billie Eilish Explains Why She Wears Baggy Clothes in New Calvin Klein Ad." *iHeartRadio,* May 9, 2019. https://www.iheart.com/content/2019-05-09-billie-eilish-explains-why-she-wears-baggy-clothes-in-new-calvin-klein-ad/.

PopBase (@PopBase). "Billie Eilish on her Grammy wins: "I love the Grammys so much but to be sitting in a room full of your idols and have them lowkey resent you was very upsetting for me and then having those people's entire fandoms that I've been a part of for years, hate me." Twitter, September 17, 2020. https://twitter.com/PopBase/status/1306661227217600513.

Pykeren, Sam Van. "Billie Eilish's Mouthful of an Album Is an Overdramatic Tumblr Post Brought to Life." *Mother Jones,* April 5, 2019. https://www.motherjones.com/media/2019/04/billie-eilishs-mouthful-of-an-album-is-an-overdramatic-tumblr-post-brought-to-life/.

Reilly, Nick. "Billie Eilish Reveals Plans for Eco-friendly World Tour." *NME,* September 30, 2019. https://www.nme.com/news/music/billie-eilish-reveals-plans-for-eco-friendly-world-tour-2552272.

Roffman, Michael. "Dave Grohl on Billie Eilish: 'the Same Thing Is Happening with Her That Happened with Nirvana in 1991'." *Consequence of Sound,* February 13, 2019. https://consequenceofsound.net/2019/02/dave-grohl-billie-eilish-nirvana/.

Steele, Anne. "Billie Eilish Has No Major Radio Hits. But She Does Have the No. 1 Album." *The Wall Street Journal,* April 9, 2019. https://www.wsj.com/articles/billie-eilishs-no-1-album-debut-followed-unusual-strategy-no-hit-singles-11554723001.

Suisman, David. *Selling Sounds: The Commercial Revolution in American Music.* Cambridge: Harvard University Press, 2009.

Taruskin, Richard. *The Oxford History of Western Music.* Vols. 1 & 2. Oxford: Oxford University Press, 2010.

The Music Network Staff. "Becoming Billie: How Apple Music and Spotify Helped Make Billie Eilish Music's New Gen Z Superstar." *The Music Network,* April 2, 2019. https://themusicnetwork.com/becoming-billie-how-apple-music-and-spotify-helped-make-billie-eilish-musics-new-gen-z-superstar/.

Weiner, Jonah. "Lorde's Teenage Dream." *Rolling Stone,* October 28, 2013. https://www.rollingstone.com/music/music-news/lordes-teenage-dream-75595/.

Wilson, Carl. "Billie Eilish's Debut Announces the Arrival of a New Kind of Teen Pop Star." *Slate Magazine,* March 29, 2019. https://slate.com/culture/2019/03/billie-eilish-album-review-when-we-all-fall-asleep.html.

Zellner, Xander. "Billie Eilish Earns First Hot 100 Top 10, Breaks Record for Most Simultaneous Hits among Women." *Billboard,* April 9, 2019. https://www.billboard.com/articles/columns/chart-beat/8506406/billie-eilish-earns-first-hot-100-top-10.

K-POP THE POLYLITH: CULTURAL EMPATHY THROUGH COMMERCIAL ESCAPISM

Buckley, Adam. "Can We Stop Pretending K-pop is Popular?" *Digital Music News,* June 21, 2018. https://www.digitalmusicnews.com/2018/06/21/stop-pretending-k-pop-popular/.

Gruger, William. "PSY's 'Gangnam Style' Hits 1 Billion Views on YouTube." *Billboard,* January 21, 2012. https://www.billboard.com/articles/columns/k-town/1481275/psys-gangnam-style-hits-1-billion-views-on-youtube.

Hickey, Dave. *Perfect Wave: More Essays on Art and Democracy.* Chicago: University of Chicago Press, 2017.

Petrusich, Amanda. "K-pop Fans Defuse Racist Hashtags." *The New Yorker,* June 5, 2020. https://www.newyorker.com/culture/cultural-comment/k-pop-fans-defuse-racist-hashtags.

Rolli, Bryan. "BTS Didn't 'Cheat' Their Way to No. 1 on the Hot 100. They Just Beat Other Artists at Their Own Game." *Forbes,* September 28, 2020. https://www.forbes.com/sites/bryanrolli/2020/09/28/bts-didnt-cheat-their-way-to-no-1-on-the-hot-100-they-just-beat-other-artists-at-their-own-game/#561dad674bbb.

Rolli, Bryan. "BTS's 'BE' Debut Is Going to Be Huge—but Just How Huge?" *Forbes*, October 8, 2020.
https://www.forbes.com/sites/bryanrolli/2020/10/08/btss-be-debut-is-going-to-be-huge-but-just-how-huge/#77aa17cad340.

Valge, Claudia and Maari Hinsberg. "The Capitalist Control of K-pop: The Idol as a Product." *International Centre for Defence and Security*. October 2, 2019.
https://icds.ee/en/the-capitalist-control-of-k-pop-the-idol-as-a-product/.

JON & POP: COMMUNITY FORMATION THROUGH POP MUSIC

Caramanica, Jon. "How a New Kind of Pop Star Stormed 2018." *The New York Times*, December 20, 2018.
https://www.nytimes.com/interactive/2018/12/20/arts/music/new-pop-music.html.

Carley, Brennan. "Carly Rae Jepsen Looks Back on Her Game-Changing Album E•MO•TION Five Years Later." *Elle*, September 2, 2020.
https://www.elle.com/culture/music/a33893478/carly-rae-jepsen-emotion-interview/.

Dominguez, Alessa. "Pop Music Stans Aren't Crazy, They're Having a Conversation." *Buzzfeed News*, September 21, 2017.
https://www.buzzfeednews.com/article/alessadominguez/pop-music-stans-arent-crazy-theyre-having-a-conversation.

Farber, Jim. "The Decade That Made David Bowie a Superstar." *TIME*, January 17, 2016.
https://time.com/4183603/david-bowie-1970s/.

Garvey, Meaghan. "Pop 2." *Pitchfork*, December 20, 2017.
https://pitchfork.com/reviews/albums/charli-xcx-pop-2/.

Gracyk, Theodore A. "Adorno, Jazz, and the Aesthetics of Popular Music." *The Musical Quarterly* 76, no. 4 (1992): 526–42.
http://www.jstor.org/stable/742475.

Gray, Jazmine. "Nicki Minaj, Sophia Grace and Rosie Return to 'Ellen'." *VIBE*, May 10, 2012.
https://www.vibe.com/2012/05/nicki-minaj-sophia-grace-and-rosie-return-ellen.

Houghton, Cillea. "Kacey Musgraves' Reaction to Winning Grammy Album of the Year Is So Pure." *Taste of Country*, February 11, 2019.
https://tasteofcountry.com/kacey-musgraves-grammy-album-of-the-year-reaction/.

Hullat, Owen. "Against Guilty Pleasures: Adorno on the Crimes of Pop Culture." *Aeon*, February 20, 2018.
https://aeon.co/essays/against-guilty-pleasures-adorno-on-the-crimes-of-pop-culture.

Kornhaber, Spencer. "How Pop Music's Teenage Dream Ended." *The Atlantic*, September 1, 2020.
https://www.theatlantic.com/culture/archive/2020/09/katy-perry-and-end-pop-smile-album/615757/.

Louie XIV, DJ. "Carly Rae Jepsen and the Rise of the Micro Pop Star." *Buzzfeed News*, May 22, 2019.
https://www.buzzfeednews.com/article/djlouiexiv/carly-rae-jepsen-dedicated-robyn-niche-pop-music.

Muller, Marissa G. "Mariah Carey Finally Explains That Jennifer Lopez 'I Don't Know Her' Meme." *W Magazine*, November 28, 2018.
https://www.wmagazine.com/story/mariah-carey-explains-that-jennifer-lopez-i-dont-know-her-meme/.

Pitchfork. "The 200 Best Albums of the 2010s." *Pitchfork*, October 8, 2019.
https://pitchfork.com/features/lists-and-guides/the-200-best-albums-of-the-2010s/.

Ryan, Gary. "Inside the 'One Love Manchester' Gig – What You Couldn't See on TV." *NME*, June 5, 2017.
https://www.nme.com/blogs/inside-one-love-manchester-gig-couldnt-see-tv-2084169?utm_content=manual&utm_campaign=socialflow&utm_source=facebook&utm_medium=social&utm_term=nme&fbclid=IwAR3G5zkqx2zoDoIhIabbkpKdqydHAtNpGZz-i4Yiti6kWRzSAmobPyecSl4.

Snapes, Laura. "Vroom Vroom EP." *Pitchfork*, March 23, 2016.
https://pitchfork.com/reviews/albums/21683-vroom-vroom-ep/.

Stanford Encyclopedia of Philosophy, Spring 2019 ed., s.v. "Aesthetic Judgment." Metaphysics Research Lab, Stanford University, 2019.

Stanford Encyclopedia of Philosophy, Winter 2015 ed., s.v. "Theodor W. Adorno." Metaphysics Research Lab, Stanford University, 2015.

Taruskin, Richard. *The Oxford History of Western Music*. Vols. 1 & 2. Oxford: Oxford University Press, 2010.

Twitchell, James B. *Lead Us into Temptation: The Triumph of American Materialism*. New York: Columbia University Press, 1999.

Vena, Jocelyn. "Lady Gaga Inspired by Princess Diana, Faith No More." *MTV*, September 2, 2009.
http://www.mtv.com/news/1620578/lady-gaga-inspired-by-princess-diana-faith-no-more/.

Volpe, Allie. "'Leave Britney Alone': Chris Crocker 10 Years Later." *Rolling Stone*, September 13, 2017.
https://www.rollingstone.com/culture/culture-features/leave-britney-alone-chris-crocker-10-years-later-111918/.

SEIZING THE SUBJECTIVE: THE EVOLUTION OF MUSIC CRITICISM
Asher-Perrin, Emmet. "For Love of Art and the Education of a Critic: Ratatouille." *Tor.com*, June 18, 2012.
https://www.tor.com/2012/06/18/for-love-of-art-and-the-education-of-a-critic-ratatouille/.

Burgos, Jenzia (@jenziaburgos). 2020. "If you don't know the history of Black artists behind your favorite music, you don't really know your favorite music." Instagram photo, June 4, 2020.
https://www.instagram.com/p/CBBYMINjC6E/.

Cohen, Alina. "The Ongoing Influence of Frank O'Hara, the Art World's Favorite Poet." *Artsy*, April 3, 2018.
https://www.artsy.net/article/artsy-editorial-ongoing-influence-frank-ohara-art-worlds-favorite-poet.

Coscarelli, Joe. "The Only Music Critic Who Matters (if You're Under 25)." *The New York Times,* September 30, 2020.
https://www.nytimes.com/2020/09/30/arts/music/anthony-fantano-the-needle-drop.html.

Crow, Thomas E. *Diderot on Art, Volume I: The Salon of 1765 and Notes on Painting.* New Haven: Yale University Press, 1995.

Dupree, Mary Herron. "'Jazz,' the Critics, and American Art Music in the 1920s." *American Music* Vol. 4, No. 3 (1986): 287–301.
https://www.jstor.org/stable/3051611?seq=1.

Gaca, Anna. "What Does the Rolling Stone and Billboard Deal Mean for Music Fans?" *Pitchfork,* October 1, 2020.
https://pitchfork.com/thepitch/what-does-the-rolling-stone-and-billboard-deal-mean-for-music-fans/.

Petrusich, Amanda. "Justin Timberlake Sells Optimism at the Oscars." *The New Yorker,* February 27, 2017.
https://www.newyorker.com/culture/culture-desk/the-corporate-optimism-of-justin-timberlake-at-last-nights-oscars.

Petrusich, Amanda. "The 2017 Grammys Have No Answers." *The New Yorker,* February 13, 2017.
https://www.newyorker.com/culture/culture-desk/the-2017-grammys-have-no-answers.

Petrusich, Amanda. "Why the Chicks Dropped Their 'Dixie'." *The New Yorker,* July 13, 2020.
https://www.newyorker.com/magazine/2020/07/20/why-the-chicks-dropped-their-dixie.

Powers, Ann. "Entry 7: Fine, I'll Write about What Lana Del Rey Said about Me." *Slate Magazine,* December 19, 2019.
https://slate.com/culture/2019/12/lana-del-rey-ann-powers-review-critics-twitter-attacks.html.

Shearer, Elise. "Social Media Outpaces Print Newspapers in the U.S. as a News Source." *Pew Research Center.* December 10, 2018.
https://www.pewresearch.org/fact-tank/2018/12/10/social-media-outpaces-print-newspapers-in-the-u-s-as-a-news-source/.

"State of the News Media 2016." *Pew Research Center,* Edition 13 (2016): 45.
https://assets.pewresearch.org/wp-content/uploads/sites/13/2016/06/30143308/state-of-the-news-media-report-2016-final.pdf.

The Black Music History Library. "Library." Accessed October 14, 2020.
https://blackmusiclibrary.com/Library.

the Elder, Pliny. *The historie of the world : commonly called, The naturall historie of C. Plinius Secundus.* London: Adam Islip, 1634.

AFTER LAUGHTER, AFTERMATH: REVISITING MUSIC IN CRISIS

Paramore. *After Laughter.* Nashville: Fueled by Ramen, 2017.

EPILOGUE: LISTEN TO WHAT YOU LOVE, CARRY YOUR OWN UMBRELLA

Burch, Sean. "How Anthony Fantano Became 'The Internet's Busiest Music Nerd' on YouTube." *The Wrap*, October 9, 2019. https://www.thewrap.com/anthony-fantano-needle-drop-internet-music-nerd-youtube/.

Burton, Anthony. *A Performer's Guide to the Music of the Classical Period.* London: Associated Board of the Royal Schools of Music, 2002.

Goodyear, Dana. "Grub." *The New Yorker*, August 8, 2011. https://www.newyorker.com/magazine/2011/08/15/grub.

Hanslick, Eduard. *On the Musically Beautiful: A Contribution towards the Revision of the Aesthetics of Music.* New York: Da Capo, 1974.

Ingham, Tim. "Nearly 40,000 Tracks Are Now Being Added to Spotify Every Single Day." *Music Business Worldwide*, April 29, 2019. https://www.musicbusinessworldwide.com/nearly-40000-tracks-are-now-being-added-to-spotify-every-single-day/.

Schecter, Emma. "Lobster Used to Be 'The Cockroach of the Sea' and Only Fed to Servants and Cats." *Foodbeast*, February 13, 2014. https://www.foodbeast.com/news/oh-lobster-you-so-fancy/.

Senner, Wayne. *The Critical Reception of Beethoven's Compositions by his German Contemporaries.* Lincoln: University of Nebraska Press, 1999.

Simmons, Bryan, ed. *Richard Wagner's Prose Works.* Translated by William Ashton Ellis. London: Kegan Paul, 1894.

ABOUT THE AUTHOR

Saransh Desai-Chowdhry is a marketer, writer, artist manager and musician who calls NYC home.

Saransh graduated summa cum laude from NYU, receiving the Interdisciplinary Academic Excellence Award and Dean's Award for Graduating Seniors for his concentration in Cultural Entrepreneurship. Throughout college, he interned at music companies such as Sony Music and Roc Nation, managed independent artists, and studied cultural criticism and musicology. He spent an immersive semester in Paris as a French minor and was a leader on campus in business, music, and writing-oriented organizations.

Originally from Los Angeles, Saransh earned a Sangeet Visharad degree in Hindustani classical music after eleven years of training.

Outside of writing, you might find Saransh curating playlists, hiking or seeking out the spiciest food imaginable!

saranshdc.com

Made in the USA
Las Vegas, NV
24 December 2020